A Nanny's Day –
The Professional Way!

*A Curriculum Book for the
Professional Early Childhood Nanny*

Written by: Kristin Laubenthal

AuthorHouse™
1663 Liberty Drive
Bloomington, IN 47403
www.authorhouse.com
Phone: 1-800-839-8640

© 2014 Kristin Laubenthal. All rights reserved.

No part of this book may be reproduced, stored in a retrieval system, or transmitted by any means without the written permission of the author.

Published by AuthorHouse: 10/9/2014

ISBN: 978-1-4685-4403-9 (sc)
    978-1-4969-4342-2 (e)

Library of Congress Control Number: 2012901306

Any people depicted in stock imagery provided by Thinkstock are models, and such images are being used for illustrative purposes only.
Certain stock imagery © Thinkstock.

Because of the dynamic nature of the Internet, any web addresses or links contained in this book may have changed since publication and may no longer be valid. The views expressed in this work are solely those of the author and do not necessarily reflect the views of the publisher, and the publisher hereby disclaims any responsibility for them.

authorHOUSE®

This book is dedicated to:

My Mom and Dad – who taught me the most important characteristics to have when it comes to being a respectable nanny.

Max, Charlie, and Grace – who inspired me to write this book. Xoxo.

Introduction:

Professional Nanny or Babysitter?

Okay, let's be straight forward here. You've all seen it. You know, the nanny pushing the stroller and yapping on her cell phone for an hour. Or, the nanny who lays a screaming child across her lap in public to change the child's diaper. Or, how about the nanny walking down the street with her three-year-old charge and you overhear her (clear down the block!) arguing with the child about what color the sky is? Better yet, what about the nanny who lets her charges loose to play at the playground, proceeds to rest on a bench, and checks on the children maybe every half hour? And the most annoying one - the nanny who screams at the top of her lungs across the museum to get her charges attention. All of these scenarios have one thing in common: Unprofessional. These people definitely aren't nannies. And, unfortunately, they are the people who make society look down on our profession. It seems like everyday when I take my charges out, I see an unprofessional nanny or child care provider toting her bored charges around. It has driven me so crazy that I had to sit down and write this book.

Some people think that being a babysitter is the same thing as being a nanny. And, if you are a nanny, you might take this as an insult. And who's to blame you? I know that I sure take it as an insult! The International Nanny Association (INA) defines the word nanny as an individual who is employed by the family, on either a live-in or live-out basis, to undertake all tasks related to the care of the family's children. The duties of a nanny vary considering some nannies take on full housework or household management duties; but typically, nannies do strictly child care and the domestic tasks relating to the children. While every job is different, the following duties may be associated with a nanny job:

- Planning, preparing, and cleaning up after children's meals

- Transporting children to/from school, activities, and outings

- Planning activities and outings or creating lesson plans for the children

- Coordinating play dates or play groups

- Keeping a nanny log book

- Keeping a developmental portfolio for the children

- Packing children's lunches

- Bathing and dressing the children

- Doing the children's laundry

- Changing and laundering the children's sheets and towels

- Ironing and mending the children's clothing

- Children's shopping or running child-related errands

- Straightening up children's bedroom, bathroom, and play areas or overseeing that the children straighten up their own room and play areas

- Helping the children with their homework

- Vacuuming areas of use by the children

- Keeping a grocery list

Just like any other job, many nanny employers have specific requirements for the nanny. For instance, a nanny might have to have a passport so she can travel with the family abroad. Families may require their nanny to have some or all of the following:

- High school diploma or G.E.D.

- Child development coursework

- College degree from an accredited college

- Governess training or experience

- Teaching experience

- CPR/First Aid certification

- Lifeguard training

- Driver's license

- Passport

- Athletic abilities

- Musical experience

- Been away from home before for an extended period of time (This is a common requirement if the nanny is relocating. Some nannies get homesick very easily and the family does not want her to leave to go home after only a few weeks or months.

- Flexible schedule

- Willingness to travel

- Comfortable working with other household staff members

While nannies may or may not have formal training, most have plenty of experience working with children. In other words, we take over for the parents when they can't be with their children. Not only do we supervise, but we teach the children new things. In my opinion, anyone who enters the nanny world starts out as a "nanny." Earning the title of "Professional Nanny" comes with experience and practice. And, if you want to be a professional nanny, you must act like one.

Professional nannies have a vast amount of experience working with children (whether it is in the classroom or at home), are CPR and First-Aid certified, have at least a high school diploma or the equivalent, and are continuously updating themselves on the latest practices in early childhood development by taking classes or attending workshops and seminars. Many professional nannies also hold a CDA (Child Development Associate) or a degree in early childhood education or another related field.

Do you have what it takes to be a professional nanny? Maybe you already are! Let's take a look…

- Are you patient? (This, in my opinion, is the most important thing a nanny should have.)

- Can you be sensitive and flexible to the needs of each child that you are caring for?

- Do you have the ability to multitask and take charge without asking the parents each and every single time? In other words, are you proactive?

- Can you follow and establish a consistent routine/schedule?

- Do you know how to use good judgment and common sense?

- Can you be creative and use your imagination?

- Are you willing to grow as a professional by continuing to learn about child development and family studies?

- Can you prepare simple, healthy meals and snacks?

- Are you willing to create an environment with developmentally appropriate activities and outings?

If you answered "yes" to ALL of these questions, you are either already a professional nanny or on your way to becoming one! Being a nanny is about being a part of a child's growth and development. Remember, you are also assisting the parents in the nurturing of their children. And not only are you educating the children, but the parents as well.

While children usually develop good social skills in a child care center, there are so many benefits to caring for children in the home environment versus going the daycare route. The child receives more one-on-one time, therefore making it easier for a nanny to be sensitive to the child's needs. For instance, the nanny can be more flexible towards accommodating a child's naptime and eating schedule. In child care centers, there are often lots of children which require all of them to follow a more strict and set schedule. If a nanny wants to put her charges in the car to drive to the playground or swimming pool, she is free to do so. On the other hand, in a child care center, the providers don't have the flexibility to gather up ten or more children and drive off. Also, in a home environment, there is less risk for developing colds, viruses, and the flu; as a child care center can be relatively a germ filled place with children getting sick often.

How to Use This Book

While nannies carry a strong love for children and have a desire to be a part of their growth; our job definitely can, at times, get isolating - especially if you are a live-in nanny. Whether you work with your charges part-time or full-time, or even if you're a temp nanny for several families throughout the year; the ideas in here will be beneficial to you. The purpose of this book is to make your job easier, diminish stress, and put a stop to boredom for both you and the children throughout your working day. I will give insight on how to create and develop a respectable schedule for your charges while also providing a numerous amount of developmentally appropriate activities from all areas of the curriculum and plenty of lesson plans. This book also encourages you to do what you know is necessary and right so the environment in which you are caring for the children is a fun place to learn and grow. While it is focused mainly on ages zero to five, there are activities you can utilize with younger school-age children. It is primarily written for nannies, however; any nursery school teacher, stay-at-home parent or child care provider would benefit from the sample schedules and activity ideas. Any nanny, new or experienced, can utilize something from this book. In the least, every nanny should know that taking care of children is about ninety percent chaos. While you will never be able to abolish ALL of the chaos that goes on in your working day, my guidelines will help you to minimize it.

You might be thinking to yourself that you just don't have time for all the planning and preparation that goes into developing a "curriculum" for your charges. That is just not true! Remember, not everything has to be big and over the top. Make the activities uncomplicated. This is especially true if you are caring for multiple children in a variety of different ages and stages. Whip up a batch of homemade play dough. Have the children help you mix and bake blueberry muffins for snack time. Mix glitter with their fingerpaint and paint on recycled paper bags to create beautiful pictures, which you might display on the refrigerator. Cut shapes out of construction paper and glue them onto a margarine tub or canister for the children to store their colorful markers in. Glue magazine pictures into a stapled construction paper book and have the children dictate a story to you. Wave colorful ribbons in the air as you dance to music. Talk about skin colors.

You see? Not everything has to be difficult. The activities I just stated take a minimal amount of preparation and planning and all have a purpose. They are budget friendly and many allow your charges to do at their own pace and independently in the event that you have to multi-task (feeding a baby, folding their laundry, prepping a meal, etc.). Remember to have humor. As long as you are having fun, the children will have fun. If you are in the middle of an activity, and your charge gets frustrated and wants to stop, then stop. Continue later on when they are ready. Modeling appropriate behavior is one of the most important things that we, as nannies, can do for our charges. Give the children many chances to make decisions, be leaders, make choices and take responsibility. Try to make it a goal that the children will be enthusiastic and fascinated in what you have planned for them. Tell them what they are doing well and be specific when you are telling them. Don't just say "good job." Say something such as, "I like how you mixed the colors together." "I like how you are taking turns with your sister." "You are such a good listener." "Thank you for helping me with…" One thing I notice frequently is that parents and caregivers tell the children what they're doing wrong, but fail to tell them what they're doing correctly. By praising a child's good behavior, it encourages them to continue with their good conduct.

Yes, in some cases, you are going to need to take a little bit of time to plan, prepare, and organize yourself. You can do that during naptime (for a short period, but not so long where you don't get a break for yourself), when the children are having independent free play (but not so long where you don't have time to play with them), or after your work day or for a bit on the weekend. I understand that we do get tired after spending such a long day with the children, but like I said, if you want to be a professional nanny, then you must act like one. Think about it – many other professionals have to take their work home with them. However, don't take it all so seriously that you never get a break for yourself. I work on my planning for a bit during naptime a few times a week and occasionally on the weekends for a little while. The best part is, after you've done lesson planning for several weeks, you can repeat activities with your charges; therefore making your job of planning easier! Save all of your lesson plans and activities and sort them into files and folders so you can pull them out when you want to use them again. I hear so many nannies complaining that "there is nothing to do" when they are working. Well, if they would develop a good schedule for their charges and come up with some activities, they wouldn't be so bored and it would make the days go by quicker, not to mention, make the days easier. It's really up to you. Impress the parents and show them that you are not only the nanny they had hoped for, but the nanny they can't live without. Ready? Okay…Here we go!

Chapter One

Planning the Day

Failing to plan is planning to fail. Period. It is very important to keep the children on a consistent and decent schedule throughout your day. This is the first step to minimizing the chaos. I believe in schedules from - pretty much - day one of a child's life. Of course, as the children grow, their schedules alter - especially with infants. Children need consistency so they will become familiar with what will come next. And with a consistent schedule, they won't be bored which can ensure good behavior. The best way to create a schedule for your charges is to take into consideration the main parts of the day, such as lunch time. There are certain parts of the day that all children, including infants and toddlers, should have in their daily schedule. These include meal and snack times (of course!), nap time (or rest time for older children), outdoor time, story time, and play time (a.k.a free play). As the children grow older, the more in depth the schedule will become because you will need to add things such as clean-up time, toothbrushing, and handwashing. Eventually, you will add school. The following pages will provide you with sample schedules to give you ideas for developing your own routine. A successful daily schedule alternates long, active activity times with short, quiet activities. For instance, many children are involved in special classes or playgroups. Be sure to alternate playdates, classes, and nanny initiated activities with child initiated activities. Diapering and toilet training should be done as needed. These sample schedules are for the daytime between the hours of 7:00 in the morning to 6:00 at night. ***Of course you will need to adjust times and activities to fit your own charge's needs as well as the requests from your employers.*** For instance, if you work longer hours, you may want to stretch your outside times. If your children take longer to eat, add more time during meals. If your boss requires that you bathe the children, add it into the schedule. If you are taking a field trip, schedule it during the outside time or nanny initiated activity time. You also may need to modify your schedule according to season. For instance, in the summer time, I schedule my charge's outside time earlier to avoid the heat. When the days are cooler, we go out later in the morning when it's a bit warmer. During the winter, when it gets dark by 5 pm, our second outdoor time directly follows afternoon snack time. Keep in mind that the following schedules on the next few pages are examples and that every child is singular.

Schedule for Young Infants (Newborns to Nine Months Old):

Young infants will follow their own unique schedule, but do your best to keep their feeding and nap times regular. In some cases, you will start a job with a newborn that has had a baby nurse, so the baby will hopefully already be on a set schedule. As infants grow, their schedules change very frequently. You will want to keep the baby on a "sleep, eat, wake" pattern. Or, at least, that's my philosophy anyway! Newborns should be napping at least three times per day. You will also find that some prefer to nap even more than that depending upon how long they sleep at each nap. At around four months, you can try and drop the third nap. (Keep in mind that when I use the phrase "around four months," I mean it could be before, at, or after four months. I have worked with infants who still take three naps up to six months old. This goes for just about any developmental milestone. Children go at their own pace.) Some infants prefer to take several "cat naps" instead of two or three long naps. Listed below is a typical feeding schedule. Infants usually go anywhere from two to four hours between feedings depending upon how much they are getting at each feeding. Some infants will take fewer bottles with more ounces of formula or breast milk less often, while other infants might prefer to take several small "snack" bottles which would mean feeding them more frequently.

Age	Schedule
2-4 weeks old:	7 am, 10 am, 1 pm, 4 pm, 7 pm, 10 pm, 1 am, 4 am
4-6 weeks old:	7 am, 11 am, 3 pm, 7 pm, 11 pm, 3 am
7-10 weeks old:	6 am, 10 am, 2 pm, 6 pm, 10 pm
11-16 weeks old:	6 am, 10 am, 2 pm, 6 pm
4-6 months old:	6 am (milk), 10:30 am (milk and solids), 2 pm (milk), 5:30 (solids), 6:30 (milk)
7-9 months old:	6 am (milk), 10:30 am (milk and solids), 2 pm (occasionally milk and solids), 5:30 (solids), 6:30 (milk)

Be sure to also fill in the day with story times, outdoor times, and nanny initiated activities when the baby is awake. The parents may seek advice from you about whether or not it is okay to enroll their baby in an infant class. At around six months old, as long as it doesn't interfere with their eating and sleeping schedule, I don't see a problem with it. Music would be the best class to enroll in at this age. However, encourage the parents to enroll in ONE class. We are talking about infants here and there is no need for an over stimulating agenda. This really goes for any age. Remember, a child's primary job is to PLAY.

Schedule for Older Infants (Nine to Twelve Months Old)

    Welcome to the movement age! By now infants usually are crawling and will soon begin to take steps. Keep in mind that some infants will no longer be using bottles at this age, so you will need to adjust the schedule to fit the developmental needs of your charge. Also, this is a good time to start using a sipper cup, as the appropriate age to give up a bottle is around twelve months. Some infants may have even started taking a cup by nine months.

7:00 – Handwashing, Bottle, Breakfast

7:30 – Playtime

8:45 – Clean Up

8:50 – Story Time

8:55 – Morning Nap

9:55 – Nanny Initiated Activity

10:15 – Outside Time

11:00 – Bottle

12:00 – Hand Washing, Lunch Time (you could also coordinate lunch time at 11:00 with the bottle)

12:30 – Playtime

12:50 – Clean Up

12:55 – Story Time

1:00 – Nap Time

3:00 – Snack Time

3:20 – Playtime

4:00 – Outside Time

5:00 – Nanny Initiated Activity

5:20 – Playtime (until mommy and daddy come home)

Schedule for Toddlers (One to Two Years Old)

7:00 – Playtime

8:00 – Hand Washing, Breakfast

8:30 – Toothbrushing

8:35 - Playtime

9:35 – Clean Up

9:40 – Story Time

9:50 – Nanny Initiated Activity

10:20 – Outside Time

11:25 – Music/Creative Movement

11:35 – Table Toys

11:50 – Hand Washing, Lunch Time

12:30 – Toothbrushing

12:35 – Limited Choice Playtime

12:50 – Story Time and Nursery Rhymes

1:00 – Nap Time

3:00 – Table Toys

3:15 – Hand Washing, Snack Time

3:35 – Outside Time

4:45 – Nanny Initiated Activity

5:05 – Playtime (until mommy and daddy come home)

Schedule for Preschoolers (Three to Five Years Old)

7:00 – Playtime

8:00 – Hand Washing, Breakfast

8:30 – Toothbrushing

8:35 – Playtime

9:35 – Clean Up

9:40 – Story Time

9:50 – Nanny Initiated Activities

10:20 – Outside Time

11:25 – Music/Creative Movement

11:40 – Table Toys

12:00 – Hand Washing, Lunch Time

12:30 – Toothbrushing

12:35 – Book Browse

12:50 – Story Time and Nursery Rhymes

1:00 – Nap Time

3:00 – Table Toys

3:15 – Hand Washing, Snack Time

3:35 – Outside Time

4:45 – Nanny Initiated Activity

5:05 – Playtime (until mommy and daddy come home)

Meal and Snack Times

Meals and snack times for toddlers, preschoolers, and school-age children should be spaced apart at least two hours. According to Gerber, twenty-five percent of children's calories come from snacking. If you are doing an early breakfast and a lunch no later than noon, it is usually not necessary to have a morning snack. However, if you feel like the children still need it and as long as it doesn't spoil their lunch time appetite, a mid-morning snack is fine. If you are not feeding the children lunch until past noon, offer a light snack mid-morning. When children wake up from their naps in the afternoon, they are usually hungry. Therefore, a mid-afternoon snack should be served to hold their little bodies until dinnertime. Snacks typically should consist of two things (such as crackers and apple juice).

Naptimes

I just don't understand why parents think it is necessary for their children to give up naps when they turn two. I truly believe that is actually one reason why sleep problems can occur. Children use up so much energy throughout the day and if they do not get the proper rest they need, it not only screws up how they sleep at night, but everyone starts off their day in a bad mood. Their brain development depends on a lot of sleep. As a matter of fact, in many states, it is required by law that children under the age of five that attend a child care center, registered home daycare, or school, must have a rest period. So, whether they sleep or not, at least schedule an hour of rest time after lunch. Besides, you need a break too! If you care for a newborn to a young infant, you should generally have at least three naps scheduled - morning, early afternoon, and late afternoon. Older infants typically have one to two naps – morning and afternoon until they're old enough to drop to only one. Toddlers and preschoolers should have one early afternoon nap. If you care for children over the age of five, you can still schedule them to have a thirty to sixty minute rest period. During this time, they can read or do a quiet activity at the table.

Outdoor Time

I have yet to meet a child who doesn't love to go outside. The first word my toddler charge says to me when I walk in every morning is "outside." He even says it when we've come inside after nearly two hours of being outside! There is no excuse to be sitting with the children in the house all day, everyday. A rain or snow storm is one thing, but a slight breeze never hurt anybody. Even if it is just a light summer rain, don't be afraid to grab the umbrellas and gollashes and go out for a short walk. We all need fresh air, so make an attempt to get the children outside twice per day if it is nice out – at least thirty minutes in the morning and thirty minutes in the afternoon. If that is not possible, then do once per day. On scorching hot days, try and get them to the swimming pool or put out the sprinkler. If the weather is freezing cold or rainy, a trip to the museum is always good. Field trips are actually social studies activities so schedule them whenever possible if your schedule with the children permits. And, definitely use them as a back-up plan on miserably humid summer days. I know in the Midwest, it gets to be frigid cold in the wintertime. If that's the case and you absolutely can't get the children outside, try opening a window for a few minutes to let some fresh air in.

Taking the children outside to run is the main way for them to get the exercise they need. There is so much obesity in the world and a lot of it comes from not getting enough exercise along with unhealthy eating. Computers hardly existed and there was much less television when I was a child – and definitely no cell phones! Now, children are utilizing electronics more than ever. Even babies should be taken outside for walks in the stroller, a push on the swings, or even just lying on a blanket in the park. Being outside really offers a lot for children to discover new things and appreciate nature. This is also the best place for your charge to develop gross motor skills, meaning they will learn how to coordinate their large muscles and increase their strength, agility, and understanding of how their bodies move.

Storytime and Book Browse

I can not stress enough how important literacy is in a child's development. Infants, toddlers, and preschoolers should be read to at least twice a day. I have always read to my charges in the morning (about mid-morning I think is always best) and again right before naptime. You might be wondering when you should start reading to your charge. The answer is simple – right when the baby is born. Some people even tell parents-to-be to read a children's book out loud while the baby is still in the womb! Sometimes children get squirmy when reading. If this is the case, it is best to read short stories with few words. An example would be one of my favorite stories by Eric Carle, <u>Brown Bear, Brown Bear</u>. It is so repetitive that older toddlers and preschoolers can even participate. Story time does not have to be for a long period. If your charge only wants to listen to one short story, that's fine. The important thing is that they are getting some literacy throughout the day – whether it is five minutes or a half hour. Allow the children to choose the book which you will read and go by their interests. If it's a warm and sunny day, take a stack of books outside and read to them under a nice shady tree. Sometimes just changing the location can help the children become more interested in reading. I remember my professor in college had a family child care setting based out of her home. She took an old bathtub and placed it in the corner of the room with lots of pillows inside the tub. She commented on how the children in her care loved crawling in there to read! In the past, I've put up blanket tents and read to my charges inside. If you are having a morning snack with your charges, read a story to them while they are eating. Finally, remember to choose books that are age appropriate. Wait to pull out The Berenstain Bears collection until your charge can sit in your lap and listen contently.

As far as the book browse part goes on the preschoolers schedule, this is basically handing your charge a pile of books and allowing them to "read" by themselves for a little bit while you finish cleaning up and prepping for nap time. They can flip through the books, look at pictures, and imagine their own story.

Playtime

Children learn best through play so it is vital to have plenty of free playtimes scheduled throughout their day. Unless your charge goes to school very early in the morning, right after breakfast is the best time for playtime (usually anywhere between an hour to two hours). Children are anxious to play with their toys when they wake up and they will do so more independently if you let them play when they want to. After all, children are most alert when they wake up. Other times for playtime might include before lunch and in the afternoon after naptime and snack time. Most nannies start their work days around 8:00. However, there are those who start their mornings at 6:00 or even earlier. If the children are early risers as well, you can decide if you want to do play time, then breakfast (7:30 or 8:00), then playtime again; or if you would rather do early breakfast (6:30 or 7:00), and then one long playtime. If you are a nanny who starts very early, it is entirely fine to allow the children to watch a half hour television show – provided it is age appropriate and they are not sitting in front of the TV all morning.

Table Toys

Simply put, table toys are an activity that the children can do independently (and without much of your help) at the table. Usually, a table toy involves working on fine motor skills or math skills. Some examples might include puzzles, coloring books, a type of toy that involves counting or sorting, lacing cards, stringing beads, play dough, letter or number magnets (When using magnets at the table, I give the children a cookie sheet to stick the letters onto), a matching game, or little plastic animals which they can sort and count. This is also a good time for older toddlers and preschoolers to practice writing or scribbling on paper and cutting with scissors. And, of course, there is nothing wrong with the children flipping through books at the table. While the children are doing table toys, this gives you a chance to prepare meals, finish a load of laundry, or finish tidying up from the morning. It also gives the children a chance to settle down with a quiet activity.

Monthly Scheduling

Maintain a monthly calendar to keep track of classes, playdates, field trips, appointments, and other outings. Do not schedule activities and outings during the children's naptimes and mealtimes. If you are taking the children out for lunch, or if it is a full day field trip, that is a different story. But don't push their lunch time back just to accommodate art class or a playdate. Work around it. Proper eating and rest is by far more important! Store your weekly and monthly plan sheets in a folder or binder where both you and the parents can see it. Also, include in the calendar if you are working overtime. Look at the calendar below. Notice how the majority of the outings revolve around the same time frame in order to avoid lunch time and naptime.

October

Sun	Mon	Tue	Wed	Thu	Fri	Sat
			1 Gym Class – 10:15	**2** Story Time at Library – 10:30	**3** Playground – 4:00	**4**
5	**6** Pediatrician – 9:30, Playdate with Ava – 4:15	**7**	**8** Gym Class – 10:15, Nanny works until 10 pm	**9** Story Time at Library – 10:30	**10**	**11**
12	**13** Field Trip to the Pumpkin Patch – 9:45	**14**	**15** Gym Class – 10:15	**16** Story Time at Library – 10:30	**17**	**18**
19	**20**	**21** Playdate with Jose – 4:00	**22** Gym Class – 10:15	**23** Story Time at Library – 10:30	**24** Nanny works until 8 pm	**25**
26	**27** Playground – 4:00	**28**	**29** Gym Class – 10:15	**30** Story Time at Library – 10:30	**31** Halloween Party at Juliana's – 4:00	

Nanny Initiated Activities

Children are always excited to learn new things so this is the prime opportunity to teach them! As you read through the sample schedules, you might be wondering what "nanny initiated activities" really are. The answer is simple – an activity that you lead and do with your charges. While nannies can be a bit less structured than a school teacher, the importance of planning new activities should not be overlooked. When I say structured, I mean uncomplicated structure. You don't need to write out plans for seven subjects each day, of course; but it's important to provide learning experiences for the children to open up and stimulate their minds. Even infants and toddlers will surprise you with their abilities and what they can do.

Every nanny should have at least one activity or learning experience planned for the day whether it is a playdate, a new painting activity, teaching your charge a "letter of the day," or even just a walk to the park. I can't stand it when I ask a nanny what she has planned for the children throughout the day and she responds with, "Oh, nothing," or "I don't know." Create weekly activity or lesson plans which include learning experiences and enrichment activities. These are your nanny-initiated activities. If you work full time, like I do, plan four structured days and give yourself and the children Friday off. Now even I will admit that during the summer months of June, July, and August; I am very laid back. This is the time do take advantage of the outdoor weather and sunshine – especially if you live and work in an area that has frosty winters. Many places such as parks and other outdoor areas offer so many things for the children to do during this time, so feel free to give yourself a seasonal break too! Nevertheless, I am not saying don't plan anything during the summer months. We still have a job to do and learning experience still should be provided. I still plan one activity a day for Monday through Thursday, but it is definitely not as structured as during the fall, winter, and spring.

All activities that you plan, prepare, and present should have a purpose. For example, let's say you are sitting at the kitchen table with your three-year-old charge and she is painting with a paintbrush. Not only is she building creativity out of painting her own picture, but she is also gaining fine motor skills by manipulating the paintbrush. Do you ever play "restaurant" or "house" with your charges? Not only is this a dramatic play activity where children can develop their imaginations, but it also a social studies activity. When you are stringing beads to make a necklace, this is helping your charge to develop not only fine motor skills, but also eye-hand coordination. By blowing bubbles with an infant, you are helping him develop his visual perception and eye-hand coordination skills as he tries to pop each bubble. Naturally, when we think of doing activities with our charges, we almost always think of art and music activities. However, there are more key component areas to be considered than just art and music. Each week, your nanny initiated activities should come from a few of the nine curriculum areas. It is not necessary to do an activity from every part of the curriculum every single day (and I wouldn't even suggest that because it's too much structure) or even every single week; but keep in mind that infants, toddlers, and preschoolers should have learning experiences from all of the curriculum areas. These areas include:

- Art
- Cooking
- Language
- Math

- Motor Skills
- Music
- Science
- Social Studies
- Health, Safety, and Nutrition

Remember that some curricular areas can go together. One example would be if you are doing an activity involving peeling stickers and sticking them on paper. This could not only serve as an art project, but also a motor skills (fine motor) activity. Of course when you think of science, math, and social studies; you probably think of lessons on chemistry, algebra, or World War II. Clearly, you are not going to teach those things a young child. But, guess what? There are plenty of activities and learning experiences in these subjects for young children too! Think of mixing colors (science), creating patterns (math), or teaching the children about occupations (social studies).

Keep in mind that children have short attention spans. Notice in the sample schedules that the nanny initiated activity time slots are only from twenty to thirty minutes long. This doesn't mean that you will even use all of that time. If you are doing a more in-depth project, such as papier mache with a preschooler; then, yes, you will probably take up thirty minutes or maybe even longer. However, if you are doing a simpler activity, such as singing a new song with a puppet, you may only take up five or ten minutes. If that's the case; plan two simple, short activities for the time slot (maybe singing a new song with a puppet and doing a nutrition lesson). The nanny initiated slots allow ample time to ensure that you have enough time for whatever type of activity you choose to do.

Remember that everything is about modification too. For instance, lets say you plan to do an activity that involves cutting out and painting construction paper hearts. As you know, an infant is not going to be able to manipulate scissors, so you will have to disregard that instruction and cut out the hearts for them. Then, they can fingerpaint them. And for heaven's sake, don't be afraid to allow infants and toddlers to fingerpaint!

My former college professor used to tell our class to try to keep "cutesy" activity topics such as "teddy bears" and "monsters" to a minimum. I was confused at first on why she said this, as children love these types of things. But then I understood what she meant as her response was, "Are they getting anything out of it?" Of course there's absolutely nothing wrong with doing fun things regarding these charming topics every now and then, but make it a goal to provide the children with practical lessons. You want to select activities which will create real learning experiences. Also, don't forget that it is very important to respect the lives, interests, and culture of the family you are working for.

All of the activities and lessons that I have given in this book are my own original ideas. Although, anymore, we all know that as "original" as an "idea" may seem, I wouldn't be surprised if you've heard about or seen some of my activities that I've given done with children before as people who work in the early childhood field have to be creative! I have collected many ideas throughout the past few years as a student, teacher, and professional nanny, but I have come up with many of my own as well. You can too! Just be inventive. It is also best to test out activities (particularly recipes) before you do them with the children to make sure that they really do work. The last thing you want is to have your three-year-old charge excited to make a batch of play dough that, in the end, could turn into nothing but liquid all because of a bad recipe. (And speaking of – all of the food recipes in this book have come from www.allrecipes.com - an absolute wonderful website which provides a plethora of healthy meals and snacks!) I'm going to say once again – *uncomplicated* is the key word. To me, any activity that requires diagrams and lengthy, detailed instructions is too complicated to do with children. A nanny's time is precious – and taking fifteen minutes or longer just to figure out how to do the activity isn't worth wasting your time over. By the time you've figured everything out, your charges will have lost their patience to sit at the table and won't even want to do the activity.

There are three curriculums that a nanny can choose to use:

The Nanny's Creative Curriculum

The Nanny's Literacy Curriculum

The Nanny's Thematic Curriculum

Throughout the rest of this book, I am going to provide you with information on these curriculums, along with several planning pages for your very own use. I will also share information with you on early academics (alphabet, numbers, colors, and shapes). And remember: any lesson plan (no matter what type of curriculum it is) can be repeated.

Organize all of your lesson plans and activities into labeled files and folders and pull them out when you want to use them again. You will often find that your charges will want to do many of the activities you've planned again – so save them all! For example, some of my Christmas and Hanukkah activities are the same every year as the children do ask if we can do a particular art project or snack idea again; however, be sure to add some fresh ideas too – especially as the children grow because now they are able to do more in depth techniques.

Chapter Two

The Nanny's Creative Curriculum

The creative curriculum is the easiest way to go, especially if you don't feel like you have much time for planning or perhaps don't want to plan around a certain theme. This curriculum is perfect for busy schedules. It is simply developmentally appropriate activities from all curricular areas – except there is no theme in which they have to revolve around. On Monday, you might be baking cookies; the next day, you might be creating a nature collage with the treasures the children picked up on a walk to the playground; the following day, you might be doing an activity that involves sorting colors; and so on. Your activities should come from the curricular areas and if your child is at the appropriate age, you can introduce letters, numbers, shapes, and/or colors. As I said, during the summer months, I'm very laid back with the children. I generally use the creative curriculum during the months of June, July, and August or if I have a short week with the children any other time during the year. For infants and young toddlers; make plans to introduce and read new books, create sensory experiences, sing songs, and recite fingerplays. Field trips are always welcome in any curriculum – including the creative curriculum! And if the children enjoy one activity that you plan, prepare, and present; feel free to repeat it the next day or week. Especially if it is something that took you some time to prepare beforehand. Sometimes, I will think up and make a neat game for the children and we will use it as our activity for two or three days in a row. See the lesson plans below for a sample creative curriculum plan for four weeks. I have listed two activities for each day for four days. You could do one activity in the morning and one in the afternoon; or one right after the other in the morning or afternoon. If you have a chaotic and hectic day; just plan for one activity.

Week One:

Monday:

    Science: Celery Experiment – Set out four small glasses of water. Drop a few drops of red food coloring into one glass, yellow into another, blue into another, and green into the last. Place a stalk of celery in each glass. Observe what happens throughout the course of the week. The tops of the celery stalks should change to the color in the glass.

    Nutrition: Fruits and Vegetables – Talk to the children about fruits and vegetables. Tell them that vegetables grow in the ground and fruits grow on trees. Explain that they are healthy food choices. Flip through old magazines and help the children cut out pictures of fruits and vegetables. Glue onto construction paper and label the fruits and vegetables.

Tuesday:

    Art/Sensory: Fireworks Art – Spread newspaper over the table or area in which you will be painting at. Pour a few tablespoons of paint into a shallow bowl and mix with a few drops of water. Have a couple of colors out so the children have a few to choose from. The children can scoop a few spoonfuls onto a sheet of heavy construction paper. They can use more than one color if they would like. Using a straw, blow the paint all over the paper to mix the colors together. Sprinkle glitter over the paint. Let dry and hang up for the children to see their creations.

    Music/Creative Movement: Dancing with Ribbons – Tape long ribbons in a variety of colors to an old paper towel tube. The children can wave these through the air while they dance to music.

Wednesday:

    Cooking: Banana Bread – Preheat oven to 350 degrees. Mix together the following ingredients in a large bowl:

¼ c. butter
½ c. sugar
1 egg
2 c. flour
½ tsp. baking soda
½ tsp. baking powder
¼ tsp. salt
3 tbsp. yogurt
3 ripe bananas, mashed
Pour into a greased 5x9 pan. Bake for one hour.

    Outdoor: Nature Walk – Give each child a paper bag before going out for a walk. As you are walking, pick up items along the way that the children find (twigs, rocks, leaves, etc.). Save for a collage on Thursday.

Thursday:

Science: Homemade Crayons – Preheat the oven to 300 degrees. Line a muffin tin with paper liners. Use old broken crayons and place them into each muffin cup. Place a few crayons into each cup. Place into the oven until the crayons are fully melted (will take a few minutes). Remove from the oven and let harden. Have the children discuss with you their observations of what happened to the crayons.

Art: Nature Collage – Use items found on Wednesday to create a collage onto construction paper.

Week Two:

Monday:

Math: Matching Colors – Use pom-pom balls, buttons, or blocks and sort them by color. If your charge is little, start by sorting only two or three colors. Count the sorted objects with the children.

Safety: Stop Signs – Create a stop sign out of red construction paper. Talk to the children about the importance of stop signs and what they are used for. Then have the children stand on one side of a room and you stand on the other. Have them walk towards you. When you hold up the stop sign, they must stop. Trade places with your charge and let him have a turn holding the stop sign.

Tuesday:

Social Studies: Hair – Talk to the children about the different colors and textures of hair. Maybe even flip through magazines, catalogs, or their storybooks and show them people with different kinds of hair. Talk about the similarities and differences. Give your charge a paperplate and allow him to draw a face on it. Glue on shredded paper, yarn, or string to represent hair onto the top of the paper plate.

Music: Coffee Can Drums – The children can paint old coffee cans and use them as drums when you sing songs together. Help them to tap beats to the songs you are singing.

Wednesday:

Cooking: Ants on a Log – Cut a stalk of celery into three to four inch pieces. Spread peanut butter along the inside of the celery (the log) and line raisins (the ants) on top of the peanut butter. A classic for snack time!

Motor Skills: Rigatoni Necklace – Use a long piece of string or a shoelace to string rigatoni. The children can add large beads as well. To make a bracelet, they can use chenille sticks. Tie the ends together in a knot, so they can wear their creations. (To color the rigatoni noodles, pour rubbing alcohol in a bowl with several drops of food coloring. Let the noodles sit in the alcohol mixture for a few minutes. Take them out and set them on a paper towel to dry.)

Thursday:

Language: Letter B – Talk to the children about what sound letter "b" makes and tell them a few letter "b" words (button, box, baby, banana). Pull out a container of buttons and have the children glue them onto heavy paper to make their own button collage. They can also glue on pictures from old magazines that start with letter "b" or use stickers.

Art/Motor Skills: Paper Collage – Provide the children with different types of paper (tissue, construction, crepe, cardstock, etc.). They can cut the paper into small pieces and different shapes with scissors or they can practice tearing the paper into small pieces and strips. They can glue the paper collection onto another sheet of heavy paper to create their own collage. Talk about the different types of paper that they used.

Week Three:

Monday:

Science: Sensory Bottle – Fill an empty soda or water bottle half way with water. Add a few drops of food coloring. Then fill the bottle the rest of the way with vegetable oil. Sprinkle in a few teaspoons of glitter and secure the lid very tightly. Hold the bottle up and move it around. Talk to the children about how the oil and water don't mix. It almost looks like waves in an ocean. Have your charge shake the bottle to see the ingredients mix together and separate again.

Health/Art: Covering a Cough – Talk to your charges about the importance of covering their mouth when they cough or sneeze because of the spreading of germs. Have them practice pretending to cough and cover their mouth. If you want to add a simple art project to go along with this lesson, have them draw eyes, nose, and a circle mouth on a paper plate. Trace their hands onto construction paper and cut them out. Glue the hands and a real Kleenex tissue over the mouth to represent how to cover a cough.

Tuesday:

Art: Sparkly Stars – Cut out star shapes from construction paper. The children can use a paintbrush to brush glue onto the stars. Sprinkle gold or silver glitter over the glue and let dry. Glue or tape a popsicle stick to the back of the star.

Music: "Twinkle, Twinkle, Little Star"
(Traditional)
Twinkle, twinkle, little star,
How I wonder, what you are.
Up above the world so high,
Like a diamond in the sky.
Twinkle, twinkle, little star,
How I wonder, what you are.
(The children can hold and wave their stars they just created to sing the song.)

Wednesday:

Cooking: Oatmeal Cookies – Preheat oven to 350 degrees. Soak 1 cup of raisins in ½ cup hot water and set aside. In a large bowl, sift 2 cups flour, 1 teaspoon each of baking soda, salt, cinnamon, and nutmeg. Stir in 2 cups quick cooking oats and 1 cup packed brown sugar. In a separate bowl, beat 2 eggs with a fork and add 3/4 cup vegetable oil, 1 teaspoon vanilla extract, and the raisins and water mixture. Pour the dry ingredients in and stir until well mixed. Drop by teaspoonfuls onto an ungreased cookie sheet. Bake for 10 to 13 minutes. Allow the cookies to cool before serving to your charges.

Outdoor: Collecting Leaves – Take a walk outside or to the park and collect several leaves along the way. Talk about the differences in the leaves. When you get home, set out all of the leaves and have the children pick their favorites. Spread the leaves out between two large sheets of wax paper. Use a warm iron to iron over the top sheet of the wax paper. The leaves will be secure in between the two sheets of paper. Hang up in your charges' bedroom window.

Thursday:

Language: Fishing for Letters – Cut out several fish shapes from construction paper and write a letter on each fish. Laminate or cover with contact paper if you want them to be more durable. Glue a magnet or paper clip to the back of each fish and throw them all into a large bowl. Or, place them all in a hula-hoop that is set out onto the floor. Securely attach and tie a long length of yarn to a dowel. Attach a magnet to the end of the yarn. This will be the fishing rod. The children can go fishing and name the letter on the back of each fish as they catch them. If you are doing this activity with toddlers or early preschoolers, write a body part on each fish instead of a letter. When they catch a fish, the children can point to their body part that is written on the fish.

Art: Corn Syrup Paint – Your charges should wear a smock for this art project. Pour corn syrup into a small bowl. Add a few drops of food coloring and stir together. The children can use thick paintbrushes to paint this mixture onto heavy paper. When their painting dries, it will appear smooth and shiny. Allow them to touch the sticky mixture if they want to. (This idea I can't take full credit for. I learned it in a child development class when I was in college. Gosh, I miss those days!)

Week Four:

Monday:

Math: Shape Hunt – Cut out a circle, triangle, square, and rectangle from colorful construction paper. Introduce the shapes to the children. Hold up one shape and walk around the house or room to help the children find objects that are the same shape. Or, hold up a shape, and give the children a certain amount of time (sixty seconds) to run and find something the same shape and bring it back to where you are sitting. Continue for all shapes.

Nutrition/Cooking: Fruits – Help the children think up and name some types of fruits. Talk about how fruits grow on trees and they are healthy snack choices. Show them pictures if you can or rummage through the kitchen to find the real thing to show them. If you want to extend this activity, make a fruit pizza to serve at lunch or snack time.

Tuesday:

Social Studies: Pet Store – Talk to the children about what animals make good pets (dogs, cats, fish, etc.). Show them pictures, if possible. Accompany them to the pet store to look at the animals. Talk about the responsibilities that take place in taking care of a pet. A pet store is a wonderful place to take a child any age. Older infants and toddlers love to watch fish swim in their tank.

Music: Freeze Dance – Play one of the children's music cd's. Tell them when the music is on; they are to dance around the room. When the music stops, they are to freeze until the music starts playing again. Continue as long as the children are interested. For added fun, give the children ribbons to wave around the room and dance with.

Wednesday:

Cooking: Kabobs – Cut chunks of cheese, grapes, apples, strawberries, kiwi, or other fruits and vegetables and place them into separate bowls. The children can carefully poke each piece of food onto a skewer to make their own kabob for snack time.

Motor Skills/Art/Math: Fruit Loop Rainbow – Give your charges a bowl of fruit loops and name the colors of the fruit loops. Draw a large rainbow onto a sheet of heavy white paper or print off a black and white rainbow pattern off of the computer. The children can then use their pincer fingers to glue and place the fruit loops onto the paper to create a colorful rainbow. If your charges are actually sorting the fruit loops by color as they do this activity, then they are also being engaged in a math lesson.

Thursday:

Science: Sinking and Floating – Place a basin of water out onto the kitchen table or counter. Help the children hunt for small waterproof objects and place them into a big bowl. Talk to your charges about how things sink and float ("Sinking means the object will go to the bottom. Floating means the object will stay on top.") Place one object at a time into the water to determine if it will sink or float.

Art: Egg Carton Caterpillar – Talk to the children about how caterpillars turn into butterflies. You can familiarize them with the life cycle. Cut one strip of an egg carton and allow the children to paint it with their paintbrushes. Let dry and glue on wiggle eyes.

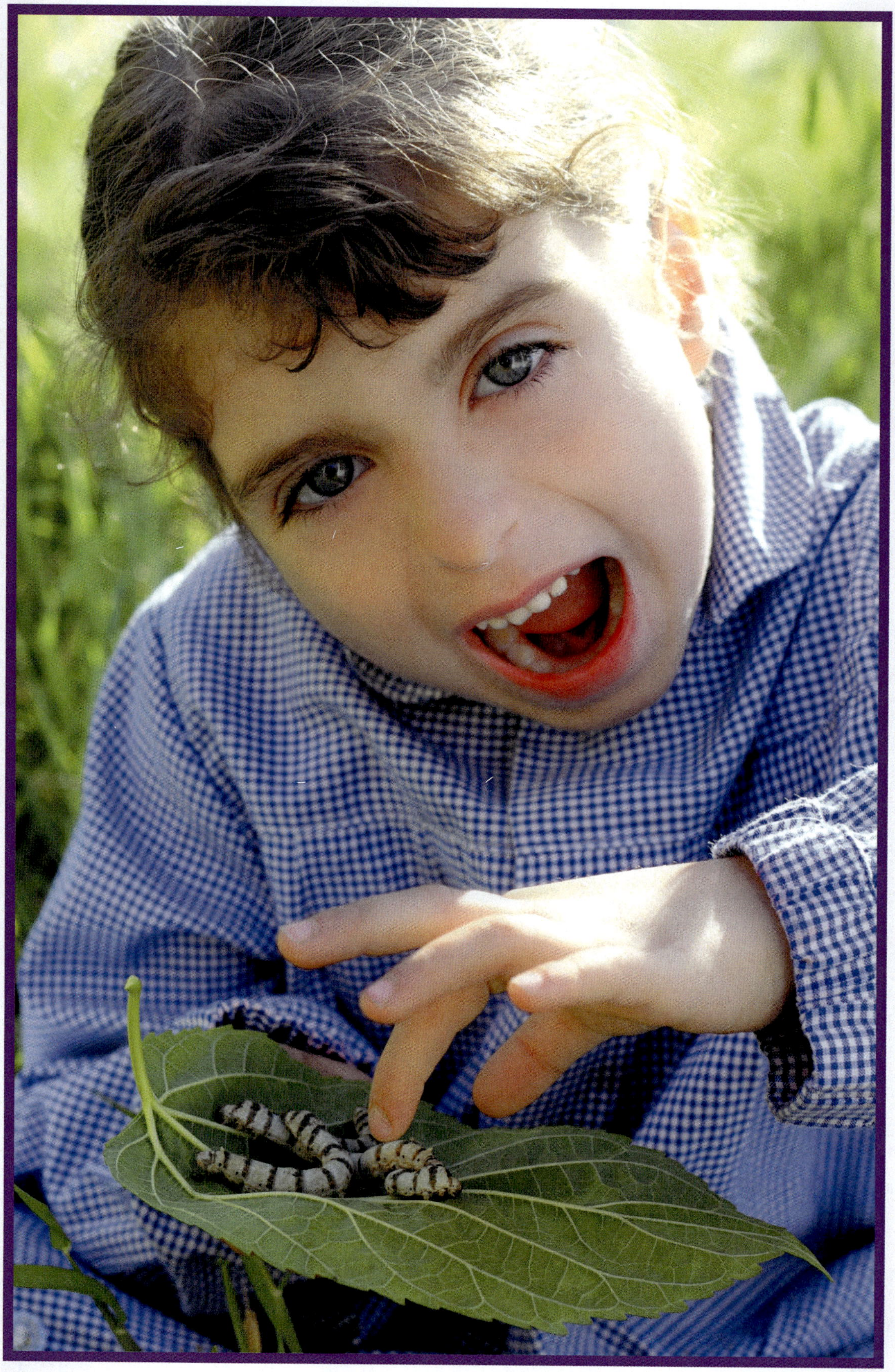

Chapter Three

The Nanny's Literacy Curriculum

By now you should know that literacy is exceptionally important in a child's development. To me, it is the most important curricular area. One way to get children eager about reading is to do follow-up activities after reading the story. The activities should be related to the book in which you had just read. For example, if you read a story about butterflies, your activity might be making tissue paper butterflies. If you read a story about going to the grocery store, you might have the children flip through old magazines and cut out pictures of food to glue on to create a collage. Or you might even take a field trip to the grocery store and point out the different areas of the store (produce section, dairy section, check-out area, etc.).

Literacy themes are an easy way to go about your planning. The week before, you could set out four stories that you want to read for Monday, Tuesday, Wednesday, and Thursday (one story per day). Then, come up with a corresponding activity for each story. Another option would be to choose a book as your weekly theme. Read the story and do corresponding activities relating to that one book throughout the whole week. Now how easy is that? Choose books that are in season. If it is July, don't select a literacy theme based on a story about snow or Valentines Day. I like to do literacy themes on short weeks or weeks when I feel like I just need a break. Or, you can make it part of the creative curriculum. Take a look at the subsequent literacy lesson plans. I have incorporated a few learning experiences for each book listed so you can easily adapt for a lengthy, short, or day by day theme.

Creative Dramatics and Incorporating Music with Books:

Some children love to just sit in a lap with a nice long story. Other children love to get involved with the story you're reading. One way to get them drawn in is to have them act out the story, also known as creative dramatics. Creative drama serves as an excellent language activity and helps the children learn to listen to the story and follow the events happening throughout the story. This is perfect for children who can't seem to sit still through a story. Take for example the book, <u>Five Little Monkeys Jumping on the Bed</u> by Eileen Christelow. As the words are read, the children can jump to the story, and pretend to fall off of the bed and bump their heads. You can play the part of "Mama Monkey" and pretend to call the doctor. This story is also so repetitive, that the children might even recite it with you. The following books are some of my favorite in regards to creative dramatics:

- <u>Ready, Set Skip</u> by Jane O'Connor

- <u>From Head to Toe</u> by Eric Carle

- <u>Here Are My Hands</u> by Bill Martin Jr. and John Archambault

- <u>We're Going on a Bear Hunt</u> by Michael Rosen and Helen Oxenbury

- <u>Froggy Gets Dressed</u> by Jonathan London

- <u>Toes, Ears, and Nose</u> by Marion Dane Bauer

- <u>Watch Me Dance</u> by Andrea and Brian Pinkley

- <u>Copycat Charlie</u> by Marcus Pfister
- <u>Barnyard Dance</u> by Sandra Boynton
- <u>Who Hops?</u> by Katie Davis

Another way to get the children involved is by singing to a book. This is pretty simplified. There are many books that are written to sing with. Take <u>The Wheels on the Bus</u> by Raffi, for an example. The children can sing the song with you as you read the story. This is an excellent way to incorporate music, language, and literacy – particularly for infants and young toddlers who are limited to in-depth activities. Try these books for incorporating music with your story:

- <u>Spider on the Floor</u> by Raffi
- <u>Baby Belluga</u> by Raffi
- <u>Five Little Ducks</u> by Raffi
- <u>Down by the Bay</u> by Raffi
- <u>This Little Light of Mine</u> by Raffi
- <u>Miss Mary Mack</u> by MaryAnn Hoberman and Nadia Bernard Westcott
- <u>Twinkle, Twinkle Little Star</u> by Sylvia Long
- <u>Hush Little Baby</u> by Sylvia Long
- <u>Hokey, Pokey Elmo</u> by Abigail Tabby
- <u>Ten in the Bed</u> by Penny Dale
- <u>Seals on the Bus</u> by Lenny Hort (My personal favorite!)

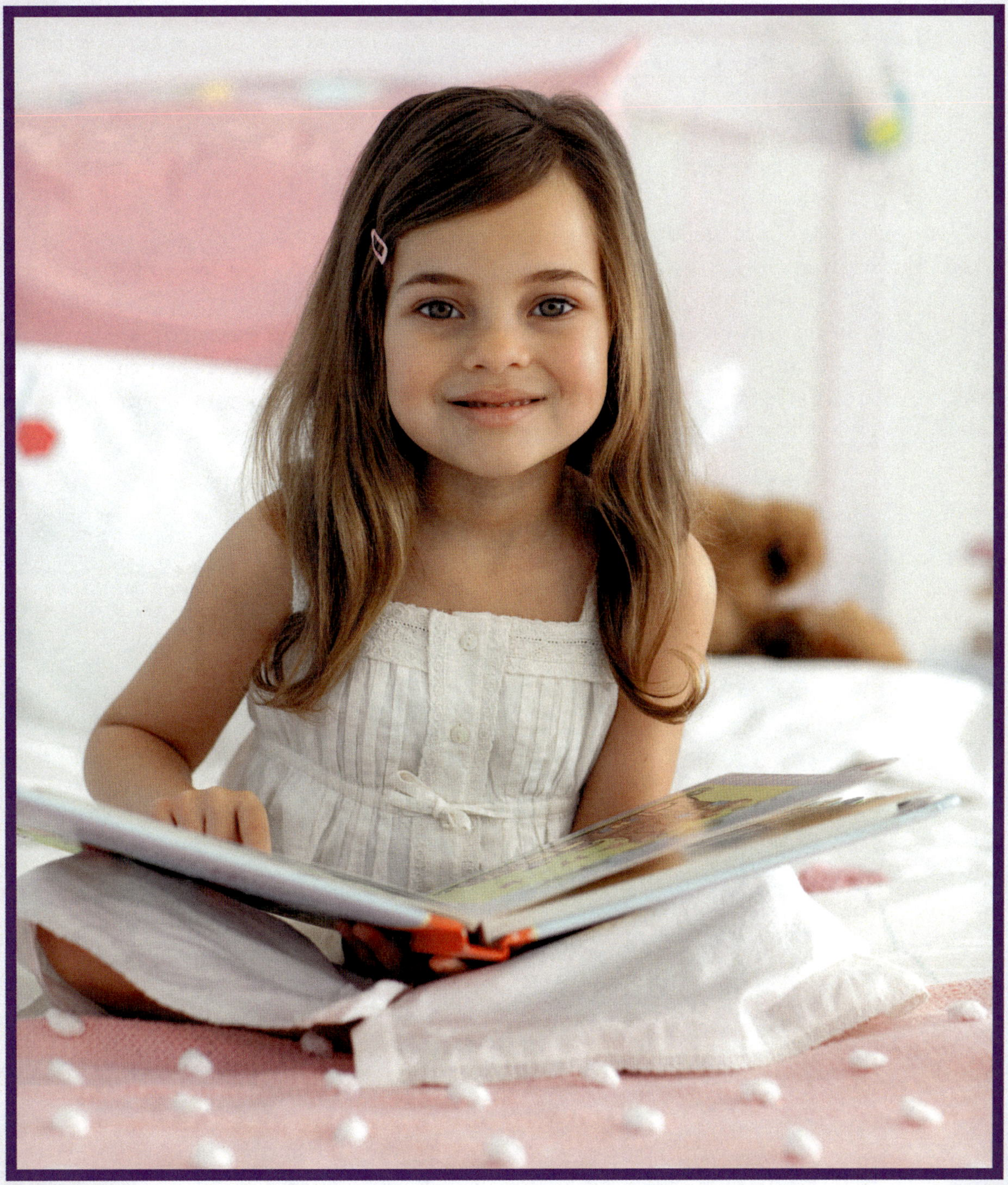

Book Title: <u>Chicka Chicka Boom Boom</u>

Author: Lois Ehlert

Follow-up Activities:

Cooking: Letter Pretzels – Buy premade breadstick dough at the grocery store (or you can make your own dough). Help the children shape the dough into letters. Place on a cookie sheet and bake according to package directions. Serve with pizza sauce for a snack!

Language: Letter Tree – Draw a large tree on a piece of tagboard or sheet of paper. Glue on felt letters or attach letter stickers to the tree. Sing the ABC song.

Language and Motor Skills: Alphabet Book – Help the children cut out pictures of objects from old magazines. Write a capital and lower case letter at the top of a sheet of paper (for example – Bb). This will help the children distinguish both upper and lower case. Do this for all letters. Cut out a picture for each page and use glue sticks to affix the picture to the appropriate letter page. Label the picture using a marker. After the pages have dried, the children can help you systematize the pages in correct order. Then staple them into a book. As you flip through the book, work on letter sounds with the children for each representation that you have.

Book Title: Commotion in the Ocean

Author: Giles Andreae

Follow-up Activities:

Art: Paperplate Jellyfish – Cut a paperplate in half. (You will only need one half for the jellyfish.) Draw or glue wiggle eyes at the top near the round part of the plate. Along the straight edge at the bottom, attach several streamer "legs."

Cooking: Fish Sandwiches – Press a fish shaped cookie cutter into two slices of bread. Scoop a dollop of tuna between the two fish to make a tuna sandwich for lunchtime or snacktime.

Motor Skills: Foam Fish – Cut a fish shape out of foam sheets and decorate with glitter and sequins. Attach a popsicle stick to the back to create a puppet. Cut out and decorate several of these to make a fish family.

Sensory: Sand Play – Pour sand into a large tub and use small shovels, funnels, and containers to practice scooping and pouring. Hide small rubber ocean creature toys in the sand for the children to find.

Book Title: From Head to Toe

Author: Eric Carle

Follow-up Activities:

Language/Creative Dramatics: Acting out the story – Read the story and have the children act out the motions, which the animals do. Another version would be to assign each child a couple of the animals. When you get to the page with their particular animal, they can act out the motion.

Language/Science: Life Size Bodies – Lay out a long roll of paper on the floor (or tape several newspapers together). Trace child's body and cut out their body shape. Have them paint or color on clothes and facial features, or dress the body up in their real clothes. Write body parts on strips of paper. Tape the strips onto the body to label the parts. You can also do this outside by tracing the child's outline with sidewalk chalk.

Music: "Head, Shoulders, Knees, and Toes"
(Traditional)
Head, shoulders, knees, and toes.
Knees and toes.
Head, shoulders, knees and toes,
Knees and toes.
Eyes and ears
And mouth and nose.
Head, shoulders, knees, and toes.
Knees and toes.

Book Title: It's Okay to be Different

Author: Todd Parr

Follow-up Activities:

Art: Name Pennants – Cut out a pennant shape out of foam or felt sheets. Use letter stickers or pre-cut letters to spell out the child's name. Glue small objects or stickers onto the pennant to represent the child and the things they like. Cut slits on the side of the pennant and slide a dowel through. Tie ribbons to the top of the dowel.

Cooking: English Muffin Faces – Toast an English muffin to firm it up. Spread butter or pizza sauce on the muffin and create a face using cheese for hair, raisins for eyes, licorice for a mouth, etc.

Social Studies: Differences and Similarities in People – Talk with the children about the differences in people. Use old catalogs to cut out pictures of people from different cultures and nationalities. Point out the similarities and differences in clothing and skin color. Include children with special needs as well. Glue or tape the pictures onto a sheet of paper. This is a respectable time to make use of multicultural dolls and books too. Talk to the children about how every person is made different.

Book Title: Jamberry

Author: Bruce Degen

Follow-up Activities:

Art/Motor Skills: Berry Bush – Explain to the children that a berry is a fruit and they grow on bushes. Draw a large bush onto a sheet of construction paper. Glue pom-poms onto the bush to represent different berries (black for blackberries, blue for blueberries, etc.)

Cooking: Homemade Jam – Mash 4 c. strawberries, 2 c. raspberries, and 1 c. blueberries. Stir in one ¾ oz. package powdered pectin. Let stand 10 minutes. Stir often. Pour into a saucepan and boil over medium heat. Cook and stir one minute while boiling. Fill jars or freezer containers and store in fridge until jam is set. Store one in fridge and the remainder in the freezer.

Science: Tasting Berries – In advance, buy a few types of berries at the grocery store. Have the children name different kinds of berries, including the ones mentioned in the story. Bring out the berries you previously purchased and allow the children to taste them.

Book Title: Little Cloud

Author: Eric Carle

Follow-up Activities:

Art/Sensory: Cloud Paint – Spray shaving cream into a bowl and stir in a few teaspoons of glue. Add food coloring if desired. The children can use this paint on construction paper. When it dries, it will have a soft and fluffy texture.

Math: Matching Raindrops to Clouds – Cut out five to ten cloud shapes and label each one with a numeral. Cut out several raindrops. The children can put the corresponding number of raindrops under each cloud.

Motor Skills: Cottonball Clouds – Provide the children with large cut-outs in several different shapes and glue cottonballs onto them. Make sure one of the shapes is an actual cloud. Have the children recite their own version of Little Cloud using the shapes they have covered.

Music: "Floating Clouds"
(Tune: "Frère Jacques")
Floating clouds,
Floating clouds,
In the sky,
In the sky.
Lots of different shapes,
Lots of different shapes,
As they float by.
As they float by.

Book Title: Ten Little Fish

Author: Audrey Wood and Bruce Wood

Follow-up Activities:

Art: Paper Bag Stuffed Fish – Stuff a small brown paper bag with newspaper. Twist the top of the bag to make a tail and secure with tape or a twist tie. Paint the fish and add wiggle eyes and sequins or glitter.

Math: Matching Bubbles to Fish – Cut out ten construction paper fish. Write a numeral 1-10 on each of the fish. Cut out several blue bubbles. The children can line the correct number of bubbles to the corresponding number written on the fish.

Music: "Ten Little Fish"
(Tune: "Ten Little Indians")
One little, two little, three little fish.
Four little, five little, six little fish.
Seven little, eight little, nine little fish.
Ten fish swimming together.

Science: Looking at Fish – Show the children several pictures of different kinds of fish. Make a list of what fish need to live.

Book Title: The Animal Boogie

Author: Debbie Harter

Follow-up Activities:

Art: Jungle Picture – Create a jungle scene by gluing die cut animal shapes or animal pictures cut from old magazines onto a sheet of paper. Glue on shredded green construction paper to make grass and trees.

Cooking: Breadstick Snakes – Buy premade refrigerated bread dough. Have the children roll the dough into long ropes to make snakes. Bake according to package directions. Press two raisins into one end of the snake to make eyes and a small piece of fruit leather for the tongue.

Language/Creative Dramatics: Acting Out the Story – As you read the story to the children, act out the motions of the animals (shake, swing, stomp, etc.)

Social Studies: Dramatic Play – Hide stuffed jungle animals around the house. Turn off the lights and let the children use flashlights to look around the house and find the hidden animals. You could also or tape together two toilet paper tubes to use as binoculars.

Book Title: If You Give a Moose a Muffin

Author: Laura Joffe Numeroff

Follow-up Activities:

Cooking: Blueberry Muffins – Preheat the oven to 400 degrees. Stir the following ingredients together in a large bowl:

½ c. butter
¾ c. sugar
1 egg
1 c. milk
2 c. flour
3 tsp. baking powder
½ tsp. salt
1 c. fresh blueberries

The children can line the muffin tin with paper muffin cups. Spray cups with nonstick spray and pour mixture into the cups until they are ¾ full. Bake for 20-30 minutes (or until toothpick comes out clean).

Motor Skills: The children can line a muffin tin with paper muffin cups. Give them kitchen tongs, tweezers, or clothespins to place pom-pom balls into the muffin cups. Stress the use of fingers with the tool they are manipulating.

Music: "Do You Know the Muffin Man?"
(Traditional)
Do you know the muffin man, the muffin man, the muffin man?
Do you know the muffin man?
Who lives on Drurry Lane?

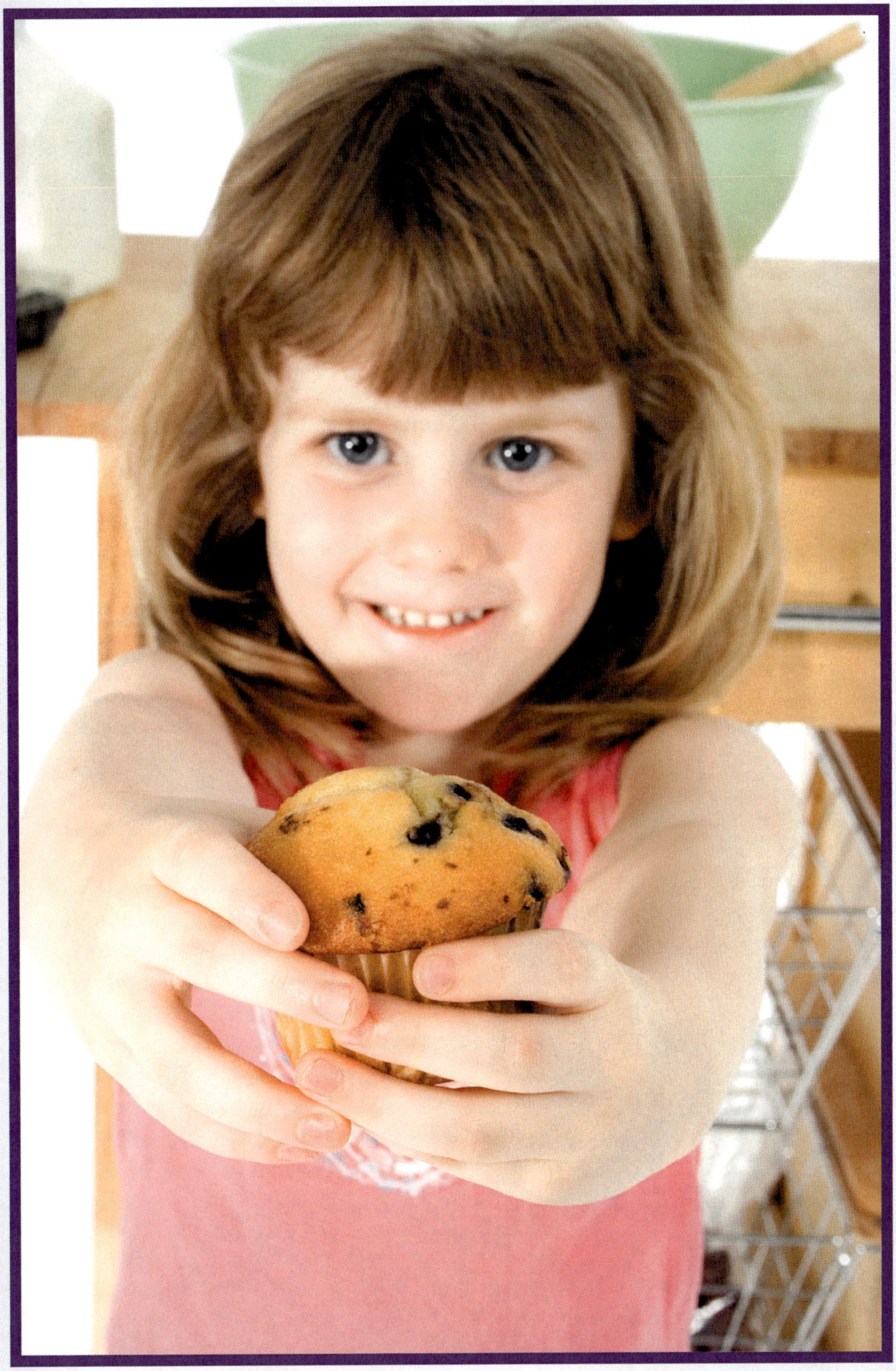

Book Title: <u>Five Little Monkeys Jumping on the Bed</u>

Author: Eileen Christelow

Follow-up Activities:

Cooking: Easy Monkey Bread – This recipe should be started in the later part of the afternoon before you leave your work day. Grease and flour a 9-10 inch tube pan. Mix 1 c. packed brown sugar and 1 (3.4 oz) pack of butterscotch instant pudding mix together. In a separate bowl, mix ¼ c. white sugar and 2 tsp. ground cinnamon together. Place 24 oz. frozen dinner rolls in the pan a layer at a time. Sprinkle brown sugar and pudding mix over the first layer of rolls. Sprinkle sugar and cinnamon mixture over the brown sugar and pudding mixture. In the microwave, melt ½ c. melted butter. Spread half of the melted butter over the first layer and the rest over the next layer. Place on the counter overnight. Do not cover. In the morning, preheat the oven to 350 degrees. Place the pan in the oven for 30 minutes. Let stand a few minutes and turn the pan over onto a serving platter.

Language/Creative Dramatics: Five Little Monkeys – Read the children the story. As you read the text, have the children act out the motions. Be sure to act it out with them! You can designate one of your charges to be the "doctor."

Math: Recognizing the Number Five – Talk to the children about the number five. Count the monkeys on the cover of the book. On a sheet of construction paper, write the numeral "5" at the top of the page. The children can then glue objects onto the paper on behalf of the number five. Pull out art collage items to start – maybe they can glue on five noodles, five pieces or ribbon, five pom-pom balls, five wiggle eyes, five silk flowers, etc.

Book Title: Silly Sally

Author: Lois Ehlert

Follow-up Activities:

    Language, Social Studies – As you read the story the first time, name the animals in the book. Read the story a second time. This time, instead of naming the animal, point to it and have the children make the animal sound.

    Motor Skills: Backwards Movement – Talk about how Sally walks to town backwards and upside down. Have the children try walking backwards. See what other movements they can do backwards – jumping, crab walking, crawling, marching, etc.

Book Title: We're Going on a Bear Hunt

Author: Michael Rosen and Helen Oxenbury

Follow-up Activities:

Art: Brown Coffee Bear – Go online to find a template or coloring page of a bear. The children can use watercolors or markers to color it brown. Or, they can just leave it white. Using a paintbrush, brush a light coat of white glue onto the bears tummy and paws. Sprinkle coffee grounds onto the glue. Let dry.

Creative Dramatics: Act out the story as you read it. When you are finished reading, see if the children can remember all of the actions they had to go through in the book.

Dramatic Play: Blanket Cave – Create a cave by putting chairs together and throwing a blanket over the top. (Similar to when you made "blanket tents" as a child.) Ask the children what they think a real cave is like inside. Use flashlights and bring in stuffed animals. I always like to serve an afternoon snack inside the "cave" when I do this activity with children.

Book Title: Five Green and Speckled Frogs

Author: Scholastic Inc.

Follow-up Activities:

Art, Science: Talk to the children about what frogs eat (flies). Cut out a frog from green felt (or use a paper frog printed from the computer). Glue a red tongue on the frog and at the end, glue on a paper or plastic fly.

Creative Movement, Music: Have the children help you sing the story as you recite it. They can act out the "jumping" part.

Motor Skills: Lily Pads – Flip through the pages in the story and see if the children can spot the lily pads. Place large pillows all over the carpet. The children can perform jumping from lily pad to lily pad.

Book Title: Busy Boats

Author: Tony Mitton and Ant Parker

Follow-up Activities:

Art/Sensory: Shaving Cream Paint – Pour shaving cream into a small bowl. Add a few tablespoons of glue and blue food coloring. (The more drops of food coloring you add, the darker the color will be.) The blue will represent water. Stir the mixture together and scoop some of the shaving cream paint onto paper. The children can fingerpaint with the shaving cream. Let dry and glue on a construction paper boat. Talk to your charges about how boats float on water.

Cooking: Banana Boats – Preheat oven to 300 degrees. Slit a banana lengthwise through the peel, making sure not to cut all the way through the other side. (Do not remove the peel.) Stuff the banana with marshmallows and chocolate chips. Wrap the banana in aluminum foil and place in the oven for five minutes or until chocolate is melted. Eat with a spoon.

Music: Row, Row, Row Your Boat –
(Traditional)
Row, row, row your boat.
Gently down the stream.
Merrily, merrily, merrily, merrily.
Life is but a dream.

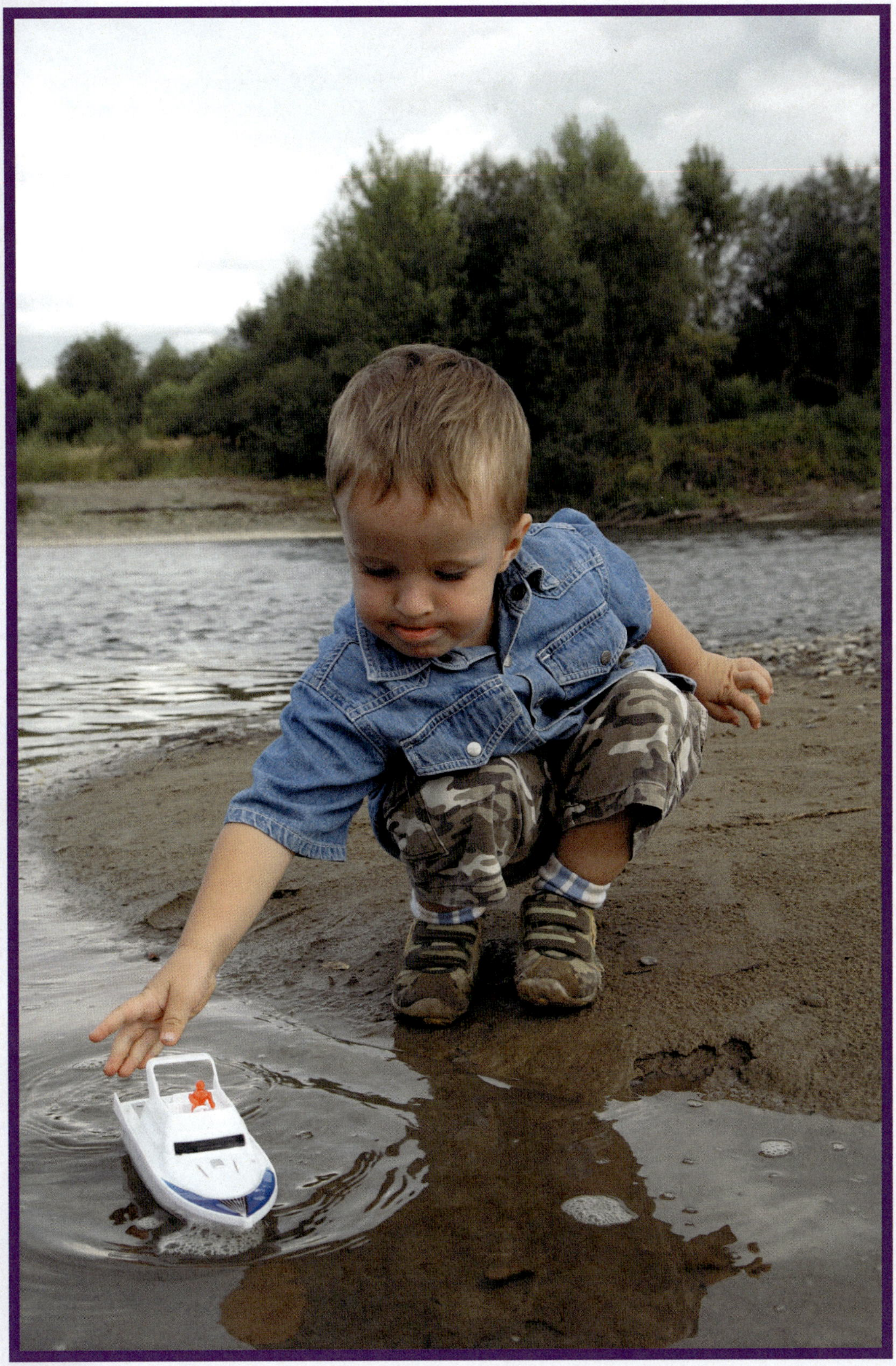

Book Title: Stone Soup

Author: Marcia Brown

Follow-up Activities:

Art: Wooden Spoons – Provide children with wooden spoons from the discount store. Spread newspaper all over the table and allow them to paint with bright colors. Acrylic paints work great on wood. If you are going this route, be sure your charges are dressed in paint shirts as acrylic does stain. Let dry and keep the spoons in the children's kitchen set for making pretend soup.

Cooking: Homemade Vegetable Soup – Combine the following into a pot:
1 (14 ounce) can chicken broth
1 (11.5 ounce) can tomato-vegetable juice cocktail
1 cup water
1 large potato, diced
2 carrots, sliced
2 stalks celery, diced
1 (14.5 ounce) can diced tomatoes
1 cup chopped fresh green beans
1 cup fresh corn kernels
Season with salt and pepper and/or other seasonings. Bring to a boil and simmer for 30 minutes. The soup is ready when the vegetables are tender.

Language: Letter Soup – On ping pong balls or recycled milk caps, use a permanent marker to write a letter. Place all of the letters in a large pot. Give each child a plastic bowl. The children can use a ladle to pull out a letter from the pot. Have them name the letter and add it to their bowl.

47

Book Title: Green Eggs and Ham

Author: Dr. Seuss

Follow-up Activities:

Art: Egg Yolk Paint – Crack open two or three eggs saving only the yolks. Discard the yolks. Add a few drops of red food coloring to the egg whites. Children can stir the concoction. Use brushes to paint onto heavy paper. When dry, the paint will look very glossy and shiny.

Cooking: Egg Salad – Boil 4 eggs and remove the shells. After they have cooled, dice them up. Add 1 diced pickle, 1 teaspoon of yellow mustard, 1 teaspoon of pickle juice, 2 teaspoons of mayonnaise, and 1 teaspoon of sugar. Add salt and pepper to taste. Mix well and serve on ritz crackers or bread to make a sandwich.

Motor Skills: Eggshell Glitter – Save shells from eggs and wash thoroughly with warm water and lay them out onto a paper towel to dry. Place shells into a ziplock bag. The children can use their toy hammer or a wooden spoon to crush the shells inside the bag into fine glitter. Have the children make a design with glue onto heavy paper (the very young children can use a paintbrush to dot glue all over) and sprinkle the glitter all over the glue design with a teaspoon. Let dry and hang for the children to see.

Book Title: It's Not Easy Being a Bunny

Author: Marilyn Sadler

Follow-up Activities:

Art: Cottonball Bunnies – Glue a small white paper plate to the top edge of a large white paper plate. Cut out pink ear shapes from construction paper and glue to the top of the small paper plate. Glue cotton balls all over the plates. Add wiggle eyes.

Cooking: Carrot Cake – Preheat oven to 350 degrees. Line two nine inch round cake pans with wax paper. Sift together 2 cups flour, 2 cups sugar, 2 teaspoons baking soda, 1 teaspoon cinnamon, and 1 teaspoon salt. Add 4 eggs, 1-1/2 cups vegetable oil, and 3 cups of grated carrots. Mix until well combined. Divide batter evenly between the two cake pans and bake for 30 minutes. Let cakes cool. If desired, help the children to frost the cake.

Math: Counting Carrots – Create five paper bunnies (or print pictures of bunnies off of the computer) and label each one with a numeral from one to five. Cut out several paper carrots from orange construction paper. Have the children match the number of carrots to the numeral on the bunny. If the children are older and more advanced, make several bunnies labeling them from one to ten.

Book Title: <u>Freight Train</u>

Author: Donald Crews

Follow-up Activities:

Art: Train – Cut out three large rectangles from foam or felt sheets. The children can glue them together. Tell them to decorate their train using sequins, yarn, or stickers. Add black round wheels at the bottom.

Cooking: Train Wheel Pasta – Cook three cups of wagon wheel pasta according to package directions. In a large bowl, beat one egg, ½ teaspoon salt, 1/8 teaspoon minced garlic, and 1/8 teaspoon ground pepper. Add ½ pound ground beef and mix well. Sprinkle with 2 tablespoons graded Parmesan cheese and 2 tablespoons seasoned bread crumbs. Mix together. Crumble the beef mixture into a large skillet. Cook over medium-high heat until meat is no longer pink and drain the grease. Stir in 1-1/2 cups meatless spaghetti sauce. Reduce the heat and simmer for about four minutes or until heated through. Drain the pasta and place in a serving bowl. Add the beef mixture and sprinkle with ½ cup of mozzarella cheese. Toss until pasta is well coated and cheese is melted. Sprinkle with another ½ cup of mozzarella cheese over the top. Enjoy for lunch!

Music: "The Engineer Drives the Train"
(Tune: "Here We Go Round the Mulberry Bush")
The engineer drives the train.
Drives the train.
Drives the train.
The engineer drives the train.
All day long.

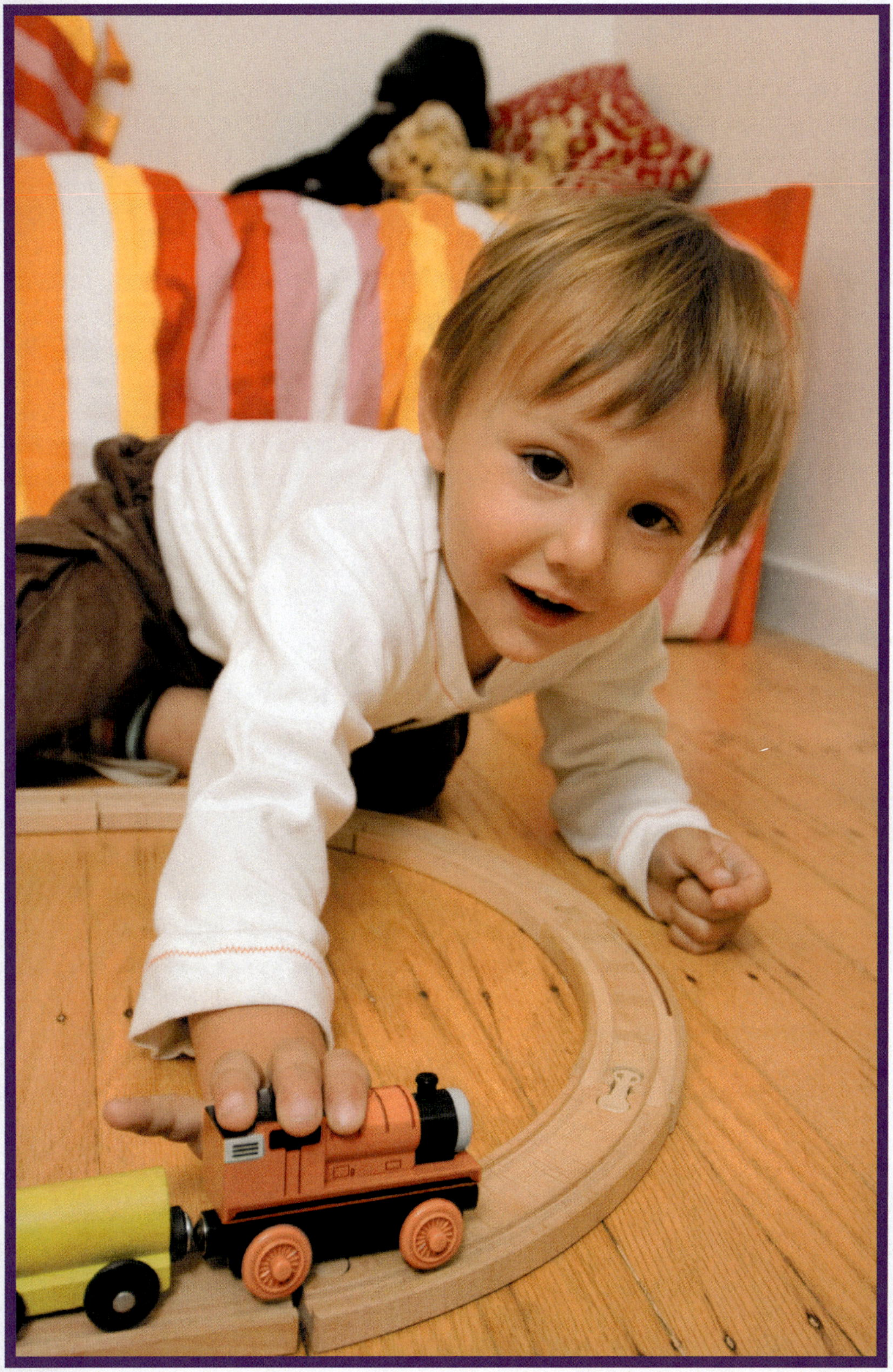

Book Title: Curious George and the Ice Cream Surprise

Author: Margret and H.A. Reys

Follow-up Activities:

Art and Motor Skills: Ice Cream Cones – Using a black permanent marker, draw three circles onto colored paper of your charge's choice. The circles will represent the scoops of ice cream. Draw a cone shape onto brown construction paper. Help your charge to cut out the circles and cones. Use a glue stick to glue the ice cream cone together. They can also glue cotton onto the ice-cream scoops and a red pom-pom on top for a cherry.

Cooking and Science: Homemade Ice Cream - Combine 2 tablespoons sugar, 1 cup of half and half, and ½ teaspoon vanilla extract in a pint-size ziplock bag. Seal it very tightly. Place a ½ cup of salt in a gallon-size ziplock bag. Kosher or rock salt is best, but table salt is perfectly fine too. Place the sealed smaller bag inside the large bag. Seal the larger bag. Shake the bags until the mixture hardens (about five minutes). Feel the small bag to determine when it is done. Take the smaller bag out of the larger one and eat the ice cream right out of the bag or put into serving bowls. (This recipe will serve only one.) Talk about the process and how the ice cream formed.

Language: "Ice Cream Chant"
First we take the cream and we pour it, we pour it. (2 x's)
For our homemade ice cream – YEAH!
Next we take the sugar and we mix it, we mix it. (2 x's)
For our homemade ice cream – YEAH!
Then we add the ice and the salt, the salt. (2 x's)
For our homemade ice cream – YEAH!
Then we take the bag and we shake it, we shake it. (2 x's)
For our homemade ice cream – YEAH!
Then we take the ice cream and we eat it, we eat it. (2x's)
We just made homemade ice cream – YEAH!

Math: Ice Cream Scoops – Cut out five to ten ice-cream cones from brown paper. Label each cone with a numeral from one to ten. Cut out several scoops of ice cream from colorful paper. The children can match the number of cones to the numeral on the cone. For older toddlers and preschoolers, practice counting with this activity.

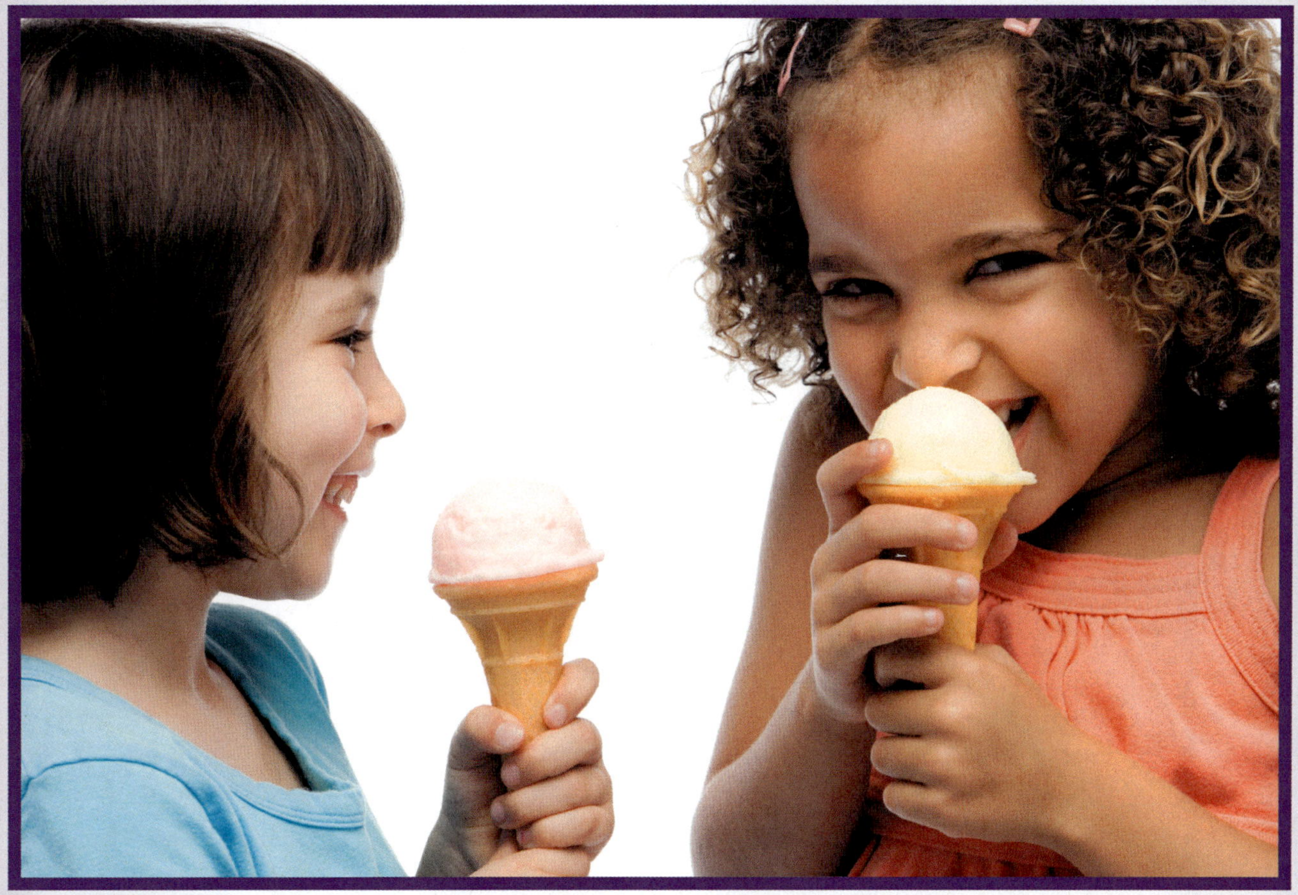

Book Title: The Very Hungry Caterpillar

Author: Eric Carle

Follow-up Activities:

Art: Ziplock Bag Butterfly – Help the children to cut colorful tissue paper into small squares. Place a small handful of tissue paper squares into the ziplock bag and sprinkle a few shakes of glitter into the bag too. Seal the bag tightly. Scrunch the bag horizontally and tie a chenille stick or a twist tie around the center to hold the bag in place (it should look like a butterfly shape. The ends of the chenille stick/twist tie should form antennas.

Cooking: Bread Butterfly – Toast a slice of whole wheat bread. The children can use a table knife to spread butter, honey, or jam onto the toast. Slice in half diagonally to make two triangles. Bring the two slices together so the top points are touching to make a butterfly shape. Use raisins for eyes and celery sticks for antennas. Enjoy!

Music: "Caterpillar to Butterfly"
(Tune: Row, Row Your Boat)
Crawl, creep, crawl, creep,
Goes the caterpillar.
He eats green leaves and builds a cocoon,
And will soon begin to flutter.

Science: Toilet Paper Cocoon – Talk to the children about the life cycle of a butterfly and how a caterpillar must build a cocoon to sleep in before he turns into a butterfly. Have your charge stand up with legs together and arms at the sides. From the neck to the feet, wrap them in toilet paper (like a mummy). They can then break out of their "cocoon" and fly away!

Book Title: Bubbles, Bubbles

Author: Kathi Appelt

Follow-up Activities:

Art: Bubble Printing – Fill a shallow container or bowl (I like to use a pie pan) with water and add several drops of food coloring. Pour in a few tablespoons of dish soap (Dawn or Joy work best). The children can stir the mixture. Use a straw to blow bubbles in the dish as if they were blowing bubbles with their straw in a cup of milk. The more they blow into the straw, the more bubbles they will get. Place a sheet of white typing paper over the bubbles and press down. You will have bubble prints!

Cooking: Bubbly Drink – Mix together your charge's favorite juices (orange, apple, cranberry, etc.). Top with ice and Ginger ale. Add a crazy straw and serve with crackers at snacktime.

Music: "There are Bubbles in the Air"
(Tune: "If You're Happy and You Know It")
There are bubbles in the air, in the air. (clap, clap)
There are bubbles in the air, in the air. (clap, clap)
There are bubbles in the air,
There are bubbles in the air,
There are bubbles in the air, in the air. (clap, clap)

Science: Homemade Bubble Brew – Stir together 3 cups water, 2 cups Joy dishwashing liquid, and ½ cup Karo syrup. Use different household objects to dip into the solution and make bubbles. Besides bubble wands; I've used spatulas with holes in them, chenille sticks twisted into shapes, a whisk, and slotted spoons.

Book Title: The Napping House

Author: Audrey Wood

Follow-up Activities:

Art: Handprint Sun – Paint a large yellow circle in the center of a large sheet of paper. Have the children press their hands into paint and around the sun to form the suns rays. Sprinkle glitter onto the sun, if desired.

Cooking: Sunshine Salad – Peel and grate two medium-sized carrots. Mix 3 ounces lemon jello mix, 1 cup water, 1 cup pineapple juice, 1 tablespoon vinegar, and ½ teaspoon salt. Add the carrots and 1 cup crushed pineapple. Mix well and chill until firm.

Music: "Oh Mister Sun"
(Traditional)
Oh mister sun, sun
Mister golden sun,
Please shine down on me.
Oh mister sun, sun
Mister golden sun,
Hiding behind a tree.
These little children are asking you
To please come out so we can play with you.
Oh mister sun, sun,
Mister golden sun
Please shine down on me!

Science: Stars – Explain to your charges that the sun is actually a star. Give them a sheet of construction paper and have them draw a large sun in the center. Distribute star stickers and press them all over the rest of the paper. Explain how stars are always in the sky, but we don't see them during the daytime.

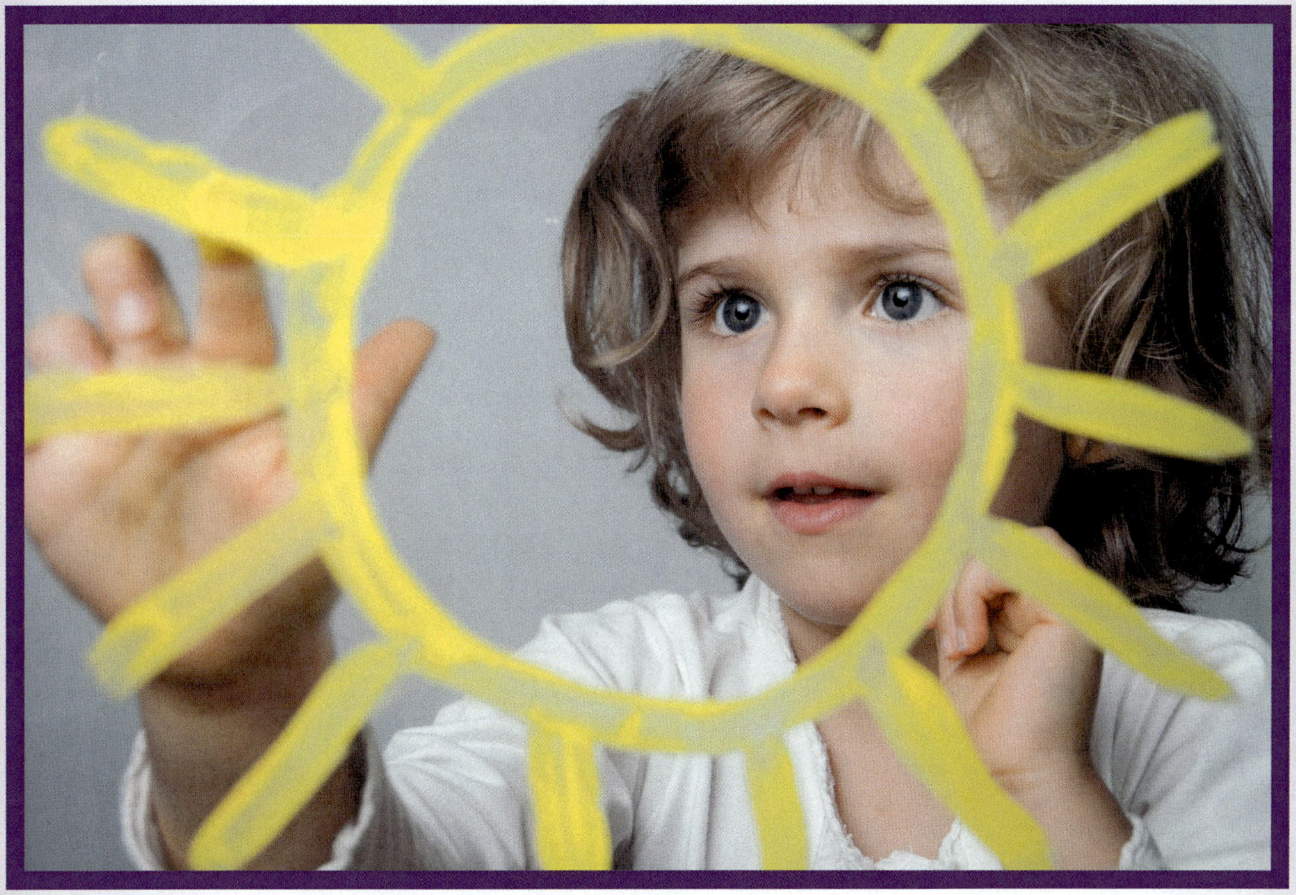

Book Title: The Grouchy Ladybug

Author: Eric Carle

Follow-up Activities:

Art and Motor Skills: Ladybug – Have the children uses brushes or sponges to paint a paper bowl red. While they're waiting for the bowl to dry, give them a paper puncher and have them punch out circles from black construction paper. Glue the black dots onto the red bowl for the ladybug's spots. Glue on wiggle eyes and chenille stick antennas.

Cooking: Bug Juice – Combine one bottle of purple grape juice and one bottle of raspberry apple juice and chill in the refrigerator. Fill an ice cube tray with water and put one blueberry in each compartment. Just before serving, add one bottle of ginger ale to the fruit juice and the ice cubes.

Book Title: The Family Book

Author: Todd Parr

Follow-up Activities:

Art, Math, Social Studies: Family Collage – Distribute old magazines or catalogs and scissors. Have the children cut out people from the magazines. They can then glue the people onto a sheet of paper to create a family. Talk to them about the different types of families. Using this same technique, write numbers 2, 3, 4, and 5 at the top of a sheet of paper (one numeral per paper). The children can then cut out that number of people and glue them to the papers to demonstrate the number of people per family. Explain that all families come in different sizes and cultures. (And, in many cases, nannies and pets are considered a part of the family! Be sure to emphasize!) ☺

Language: Family Activities – Flip through the story and have the children tell some of the activities that the families do in the book. Create a list with the children of activities that they do with their family. Talk about family traditions too.

Book Title: Career Day

Author: Anne Rockwell

Follow-up Activities:

Language and Social Studies: Jobs in the Community – Help the children compile a list of people or businesses they see in the community. They might come up with library, doctor's office, grocery store, fire station, lifeguards at the swimming pool, gas station, barber, baker, or landscaper. Go through your list with them and explain what each individual or business does in the community. Using props and costumes, you and your charges can dress up as a community worker. See if your charges can guess which community worker you are and vice versa. Books can be used for a librarian, play scissors for a barber, swim clothes for a lifeguard, daddy's white work shirt for a doctor, cookie sheets or cake pans for a baker along with a white hat, a bag of fruits and vegetables and a cash register for a grocer, etc. Get creative!

Motor Skills: Construction Worker – Get out the children's play dough and show them how to pound plastic nails into their dough with a hammer.

Music: "In Our Community"
(Tune: "The Wheels on the Bus")
The <u>dentist's</u> job is to <u>check our teeth, check our teeth, check our teeth.</u>
The <u>dentist's</u> job is to <u>check our teeth</u>.
In our community.
*Replace underlined words for: fireman's/put out fires, doctor's/keep us well, policeman's/keep us safe, baker's/make yummy food, mailman's/deliver letters, and barber's/cut our hair.

Science: Baker's Bread and Glue Dough – Tear two slices of bread into small pieces (with crust removed) and place in a bowl. Add one tablespoon of white school glue. Mix together with hands until dough forms and knead for a minute or two. If the dough comes out too sticky, add more bread. If it seems too dry, add more glue. The children can use cookie cutters and make different shapes. Let dry on a sheet of wax paper. After the shapes are completely dry and hard, they can paint them. This makes a great sensory experience.

Chapter Four

The Nannies' Thematic Curriculum

You might choose to do a weekly theme with your charges. This is what I usually do. Or, you could do a daily theme. If you are going with this approach, try to pick a theme that the children are familiar with – something that they can relate to. This will broaden their knowledge on topics that they already know about. There are literally hundreds, maybe even thousands, of options. A theme can last a day, a week, or however long the children seem to be interested. If you only have time for one nanny initiated activity per day, your theme could even go on for a month. This way, if you have a very broad theme with lots of activities that you have in mind to do with the children, you can spread it out over the course of the month. Themes can be people, places, or things. If your charge is at least the age of two, you could choose a color or shape. Preschoolers can have themes revolving around letters or numbers. If you would like to select a holiday, be sure it is fine with your employers first. If your employer is not in favor of you celebrating or teaching the holiday to your charges, and you really want to incorporate it; perhaps you could select the symbol of the holiday as your theme. For instance, if it's Halloween, select "Pumpkins." If it's Valentines Day, opt for "Hearts."

Take your cue from the children too and go by what they are interested in at the moment. My current two-year-old charge has become so interested in boats lately, so I selected it as my theme for the week. A few months ago, he was fascinated with elephants, giraffes, and other zoo animals. As a result, we did a week of learning about zoo animals and took a field trip to the Central Park Zoo so he could experience it for the real thing. Go by your charge's current events too. One occurrence would be if your boss is due with a baby soon. In that case you could choose "Babies" as a theme to do with your charge to prepare them for a new sibling. Also, make sure the theme is in season. For instance, you shouldn't select a theme revolving around pumpkins during the month of April. Just like you shouldn't select "Easter Eggs" in December!

Planning a Theme for Infants and Young Toddlers

I know what you're thinking… What can you possibly do with a child between the ages of zero to eighteen months? Almost all of my learning experiences can easily be modified in one way or another. With this particular age group, it is best to do lots of music, motor skills, and sensory activities. Of course you are going to have to adapt a lot, but believe it or not, infants can still have themes just like older toddlers and preschoolers. Lets say that your theme is "Shapes." Learning several shapes would be too much for this age group. So, decide on one or two shapes – "Circles" or "Circles and Triangles". Another example would be the theme, "Feelings." This, again, is quite broad. Therefore, make it "Happy and Sad."

In terms of art, think of having them use their hands a lot – fingerpainting and pressing their hands into paint, ink pads, or goopy concoctions and onto paper. Playdough works well too. Then again, you will have to teach them to not eat the painting materials and mixtures. I love using pudding and whip cream as paint with very small children – that way if it gets in their mouth, it will not harm their body. Bottom line – be patient with them. The next several pages will give you 24 themes and a few activities to go with each. I've made them to be for a week's length (typically four days and give yourself the fifth day off). An included theme happens to be my favorite holiday – Valentines Day! I just couldn't resist!

Theme: Winter

Art: Styrofoam Snowman – Cut out three circles from white paper. The children can use a glue stick to glue one circle on top of the other. Then, they can spread glue all over the snowman and stick Styrofoam pieces in the glue. If you don't have Styrofoam, you could also use cotton. Glue on two small black circles at the top for eyes and an orange carrot nose. Attach a scarf using ribbon or yarn, if desired.

Cooking: Snow Ice Cream - Pour 1 can (14 oz.) of sweetened condensed milk over 8 cups of fresh snow or shaved ice. Add 1 teaspoon of vanilla extract. Mix to combine and serve immediately.

Language: Winter Clothing – Talk to the children about what is appropriate and what would not be appropriate to wear during cold weather. Cut out pictures from old catalogs and magazines of things we wear in the wintertime to stay warm. Glue the pictures onto a sheet of paper. Label and name each item.

Motor Skills: Snowflake Jump – Place several cut-out snowflakes on the floor. Spread them out and instruct the children to jump from snowflake to snowflake. You can also put all of the snowflakes in a circle and instruct the children to run, hop, tiptoe, and walk backwards around the snowflakes.

Music: "Snow is Falling"
(Tune – "Are You Sleeping")
Snow is falling, snow is falling
From the sky, from the sky.
White and fluffy snowflakes, white and fluffy snowflakes
On the ground, on the ground.

Science: Snow Experiment – Take the children outside and have them fill two medium-size containers with snow. Take them back inside and place one container in the freezer and one on the counter. Have them go back to playing for a while and come back to observe both containers of snow. Discuss their observations and talk about what happened.

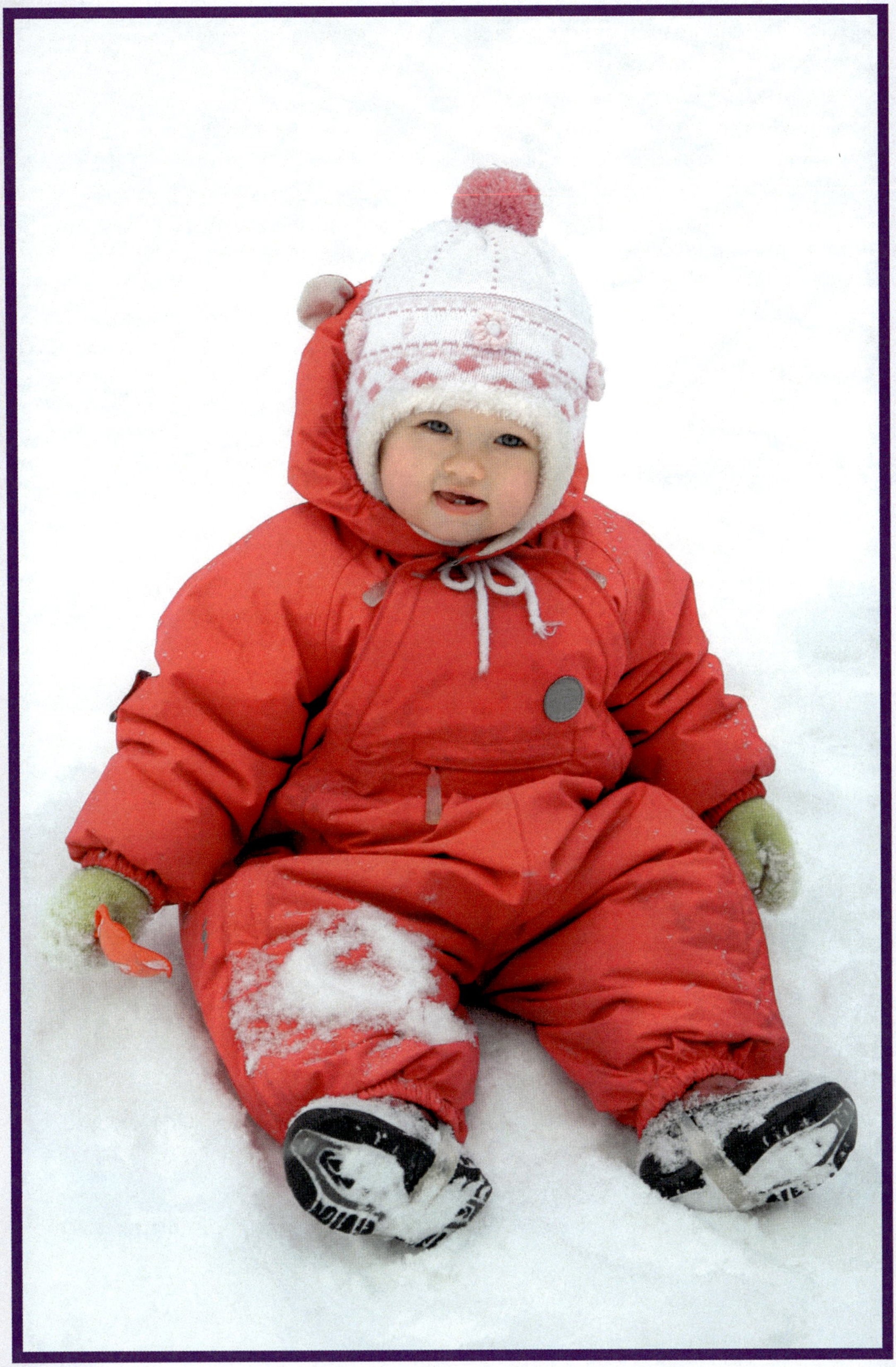

Theme: <u>Shapes</u>

Art: Sponge Painting – Cut sponges into different shapes. Pour paint into small dishes or paper plates. The children can dip the sponges into paint and onto large sheets of paper. Let dry and help the children to name the shapes they printed.

Cooking: Shape Pretzels – Purchase a package of bread dough from the grocery store. Roll out the dough and slice into strips. Help the children form shapes with the dough and set on a cookie sheet. I always sprinkle a bit of sea salt or cinnamon and sugar onto these for the children. Bake according to package directions. Let cool and serve at snack time. The children can also dip these into mustard or honey.

Math: Matching Shapes – Cut out several shapes from old wallpaper books. If you don't have wallpaper books, use printed card stock. Sort the shapes into piles. After the children are done sorting, count how many sides each shape has.

Motor Skills: Tissue Paper Shapes – Have the children use their kid scissors to cut colorful tissue paper into different shapes. Use a paintbrush to brush a thin layer of glue onto heavy paper. They can then press their shapes onto the paper.

Music: "Counting the Sides of Shapes"
(Tune: "Here We Go Round the Mulberry Bush")
Lets count the sides of our shapes, of our shapes, of our shapes.
Lets count the sides of our shapes.
Lets count them now.

A triangle has three sides, three sides, three sides.
A triangle has three sides.
1, 2, 3.

The rectangle and square have four sides, four sides, four sides.
The rectangle and square have four sides.
1, 2, 3, 4.

Circles and ovals have no sides, no sides, no sides.
Circles and ovals have no sides.
No sides at all.

Social Studies: Neighborhood Shapes – Take a walk around the neighborhood and point out the different shapes that the children see from doors, windows, signs, etc.

65

Theme: Teeth

Art: Toothbrush Painting – Give each child a large sheet of paper and a toothbrush. They can dip the toothbrush into a dish of paint and paint along the paper just as if they were using a paintbrush.

Cooking: Apple Smiles – Cut an apple into wedges. Spread peanut butter on one side of 2 wedges. Stick a few mini marshmallows on the peanut butter on one of the apple wedges and top with the other apple wedge - peanut butter side down. It will look like a smile - the red skin on the apple represents the lips and the marshmallows are the teeth.

Language: Healthy Habits – Read the story, <u>Brush Your Teeth Please</u> by Leslie McGuire. Have your charges brush their teeth along with the story. Help them to understand up, down, back, and in circles. Talk about other ways to keep your body healthy. Some answers might be eating healthy foods, drinking water, exercising, washing the face, taking a bath, and going to the doctor for a check-up.

Math: Estimating Teeth – Talk to the children about their teeth and how we should take care of them. Have them guesstimate how many teeth are in their mouth. Have them watch in the mirror while you count their teeth. Explain how babies have no teeth at first but they eventually grow baby teeth.

Music: "Brush, Brush, Brush Your Teeth"
(Tune: "Row, Row, Row Your Boat")
Brush, brush, brush your teeth
Brush them twice a day.
Round and round
And up and down
To keep your smile clean!

Science: Taking Care of Your Teeth – Boil two eggs and have your charge place one egg in a glass of coke and the other in a glass of water. Leave the eggs to set for an hour or two. When the children come back, take the eggs out and discuss their observations. The egg that sat in the coke should be brown and stained, while the egg that sat in water will maintain it's cleanliness and color. Explain the importance of eating healthy and taking care of teeth. Have them use toothpaste and a toothbrush to brush the stained egg clean.

Social Studies: Dentist – Talk to the children about what a dentist does. Go online to find pictures of a dentist to show to the children. Pretend to be a dentist checking your charge's teeth. Then, let her do the same to you.

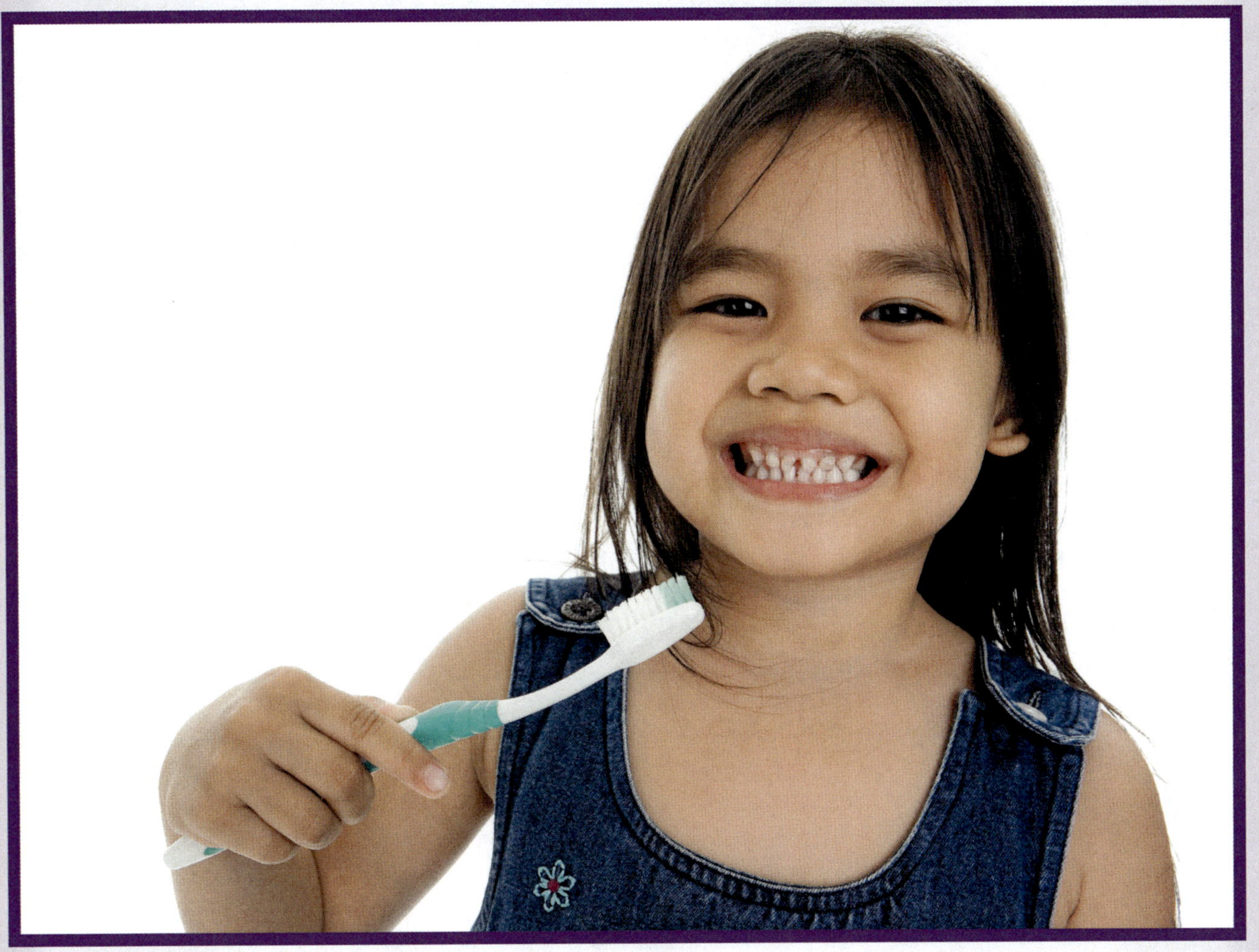

Theme: Valentines Day

Art: Sponge Painted Hearts – Give the children a large sheet of heavy white paper or tagboard. Pour red and pink paint onto a paper plate. Press a sponge into the paint and show your charge how to press onto the paper to make sponge prints. Cover the entire paper. Let dry and cut into heart shapes. If you punch a hole at the top of the heart, you can loop and tie a piece of yarn through to hang a heart on their bedroom doorknob or in a window.

Cooking: Heart Cupcakes – Purchase a box of cake mix at the grocery store and prepare the batter according to package directions. The children can place the cupcake liners in the cupcake pan. Pour batter into each liner. Before placing the pan in the oven, place a marble between the cupcake liner and the pan to make an indent. Do this to each cupcake liner. The indent from the marble will make the cupcake look heart-shaped when it comes out of the oven. If you do not have marbles, use a small ball of aluminum foil. Place into the oven and bake according to package directions. After the cupcakes have cooled, decorate with frosting and red sprinkles.

Math: Heart Match – Cut out several heart shapes in different sizes (make them all different colors). The children can line them up from smallest to largest and vice versa. For the very young children, make 3 sets of hearts (small, medium, and large). They can match them up by their size. Be sure to make them different colors so that they are learning how to match by size and not the color.

Motor Skills and Music: Heart Jumping – Cut out several large red and pink hearts. Spread them out all over the floor. Have your charge practice jumping from heart to heart. After practicing jumping from one heart to another, play a children's music cd for your charges to jump to. When the music stops, they must stand on one heart and balance on one foot until the music starts playing again.

Science: Talk to the children about the heart inside their body. Have them place their hand on their heart. If the children have a toy stethoscope, demonstrate how it is used.

Theme: Transportation

Art: Traffic Painting – Pour tempera paint onto a large paper plate. Spread out large sheets of paper. The children can roll their toy cars and trucks into the paint and "drive" them all over the paper. When dry, talk about the different materials used to create the prints on the paper.

Cooking: Stoplight Snack – Break a graham cracker in half and spread peanut butter on top. The children can press red, yellow, and green m&m's into the peanut butter to resemble a stoplight. Make a few of these for each child.

Language and Social Studies: Red Means Stop, Green Means Go – Take the children out for a walk and point out the stoplights. (Or do this as you're driving them to a particular activity.) Teach them which each color means – red means stop, yellow means be careful, and green means go. When you get back home, cut out a black rectangle from construction paper or foam sheets. Cut out three circles – red, yellow, and green. Have the children glue the circles on the black rectangle and tell you what they mean.

Math and Social Studies: Wheels – Using books from home or the library, have the children look at different types of vehicles – trucks, buses, semis, cars, bicycles, tricycles, wagons, airplanes, and trains. Stress the different forms of transportation that people use. Talk about how some vehicles have more wheels than others. The children can observe and count the number of wheels.

Motor Skills: Homemade Play Dough – Stir together 1 cup flour, 1 cup warm water, 2 teaspoons cream of tartar, 1 teaspoon vegetable oil, ¼ cup salt, and several drops of food coloring. Cook over medium heat until smooth. Continue cooking after the mixture thickens and until the dough comes together in the pan to form a ball. Remove from pan and knead until it is blended smooth. The children can use their toy vehicles to make tracks in the play dough. Have them knead the dough in their hands. Encourage them to squeeze and pound to promote working their motor skills. Store in an airtight container or a ziplock bag.

Music: "The Wheels on the Bus"
(Traditional)
The wheels on the bus go round and round,
Round and round,
Round and round.
The wheels on the bus go round and round,
All over town.

The wipers on the bus go swish, swish, swish,
Swish, swish, swish,
Swish, swish, swish.
The wipers on the bus go swish, swish, swish,
All over town.

The horn on the bus goes beep, beep, beep,
Beep, beep, beep,

Beep beep beep.
The horn on the bus goes beep, beep, beep,
All over town.

Theme: Nursery Rhymes

Art: "Twinkle, Twinkle, Little Star" – Cut out star shapes out of white or yellow cardstock or tagboard. Create different sizes. The children can use a paintbrush to brush glue all over the stars. (You may want to do this over wax paper or newspaper to avoid glue spills and other messes.) Sprinkle silver or gold glitter over the stars. After the stars have dried, glue onto a large sheet of paper to create a mural of stars. The children can sing the nursery rhyme:
Twinkle, twinkle little star;
How I wonder what you are.
Up above the world so high,
Like a diamond in the sky.
Twinkle, twinkle little star;
How I wonder what you are.

Cooking: Little Miss Muffet – Give the children cottage cheese and crackers for snack. Recite "Little Miss Muffet" and explain what "curds" are:
Little Miss Muffet sat on a tuffet,
Eating her curds and whey.
Along came a spider and sat down beside her,
And frightened Miss Muffet away!

Motor Skills: "Jack Be Nimble" – Cover a toilet paper tube or empty margarine tub with construction paper or contact paper. Glue or tape a yellow flame at the top. This will represent your candle stick. The children can take turns jumping over the candlestick while you recite the nursery rhyme:
Jack be nimble,
Jack be quick.
Jack jump over the candlestick!

Music: "Jack and Jill" – Sing the nursery rhyme and act out the words with the children.
Jack and Jill went up the hill (pretend to climb up a hill)
To fetch a pail of water.
Jack fell down (fall down)
And broke his crown.
And Jill came tumbling after. (roll down a pretend hill)
Explain to the children some of the phrases in the nursery rhyme (ex. fetch a pail of water, broke his crown) as they most likely don't know what they mean.

Science: "Humpty Dumpty" – Recite the nursery rhyme:
Humpty Dumpty sat on a wall.
Humpty Dumpty had a great fall.
All of the king's horses and all of the king's men.
Couldn't put Humpty together again!

Explain to the children that eggs are very fragile. Talk about the parts of the egg – shell, egg white, and the yoke. Tell them that you're going to have an egg toss, but the egg can't break. Help them come up with a way to "secure" the egg so that it won't break. You can use cotton, newspaper, tissue paper, bubble wrap, etc. Get creative with this! I usually have the children place the very-padded egg into a small box and tape it shut. Take them outside onto the grass and toss the egg around. After a while, open the box and check to see if the egg broke.

Social Studies: Do You Know the Muffin Man? – Sing the traditional song:
Do you know the muffin man?
The Muffin Man?
The Muffin Man?
Do you know the Muffin Man?
Who lives on Drury Lane?

Take the children to the bakery during snacktime one day during the week. They can look at all of the pastries. Name the different types of muffins.

Theme: Flowers

Art: Egg Carton Flowers – Paint the top and bottom side of an egg carton (except for the lid). After the paint dries, cut out each section (egg cup) of the egg carton. This will be your flower. Poke a small hole (nanny's job) into the bottom of the section and insert a pipe cleaner for a stem. Place in a small vase for a bouquet.

Cooking: Flower Biscuits – Buy premade biscuits from the grocery store and arrange them on a cookie sheet. Use scissors to cut six small slits around the whole biscuit. Press a small indent in the center of the biscuit. Put a small dollop of jam in the indent. Bake according to package directions. When they come out of the oven, they will look like flowers!

Motor Skills: Digging in Dirt – Pour potting soil into a large container and allow your charges to practice scooping and pouring of the dirt in and out of clay pots. Use silk flowers and chenille stick "worms" for this activity too.

Music: "Up Pop the Flowers"
(Tune: "Pop Goes the Weasel")
I planted some seeds in the dirt.
The rain fell in a shower.
The sun came up and what do you know?
Up popped the flowers!

Science and Social Studies: Planting Flowers – Take the children on a field trip to the greenhouse and have them pick out flower seeds that they would like to plant. As you look at the seeds and flowers, tell the names of the flowers you are looking at. Be sure to buy potting soil as well. Help them plant their flowers in little Styrofoam cups or clay pots. Tell them that flowers need plenty of sunlight, air, and water to grow. Have a specific time during the day when the children are to check up on their flowers and water them. Watch them grow!

Theme: <u>Zoo</u>

Art: Cookie Cutter Painting – Collect cookie cutters of different zoo animal shapes. Spread out paper and pour paint onto paper plates. Press cookie cutters into paint and onto paper to make a print. When dry, the children can glue strips of yarn or string vertically across the paper to look like the animals are in a cage at the zoo.

Cooking and Math: Animal Crackers – Serve animal crackers for snack time. The children can sort the animals into separate bowls. Help them count the number of animals they put in each bowl.

Language: Guess the Zoo Animal – Read the story, <u>Dear Zoo</u> by Rod Campbell. Have the children guess which animal is behind each flap in the story before you lift it. When finished reading, have the children name the animals that were in the story. Help them to say the animals sounds. (Teaching children animal sounds at an early age helps them to develop alphabet letter sounds.)

Music: "We're Going to the Zoo"
(Tune: "Here We Go Round the Mulberry Bush")
We're going to the zoo and whom will we see?
Who will we see?
Who will we see?
We're going to the zoo and whom will we see?
A <u>tiger</u> looking at me!
(Replace underlined word with other zoo animals such as elephant, monkey, zebra, penguin, sea lion, etc.)

Social Studies: Zoo Field Trip – Load everyone up into the car and take your charges to the zoo for the day, or even half a day. On the car ride there, talk about what animals you might see at your trip to the zoo. While most zoos are very large, try to keep to the animals that the children are most interested in.

Theme: Picnic

Art and Language: Picnic Plates – Cut out pictures of food from old magazines. (Cooking magazines are great for this activity.) Have your charges name the foods that you cut out. Or, you can print pictures off of the computer from clip-art. Glue onto a paper plate. Glue a construction paper ant onto the plate.

Cooking and Social Studies: Simple Potato Salad – Bring a pot of salted water to a boil and add three red potatoes. Cook for about 15 minutes. Drain and cool the potatoes and then dice them up. Also boil, drain, and cool two eggs. Peel and dice the eggs as well. Combine in a mixing bowl and stir in 1-1/2 cups of creamy salad dressing. Take the potato salad on a picnic with yummy fruit. The children can also make sandwiches of their choice. If you are choosing to have a picnic theme in the winter, they can have their picnic on the kitchen floor with a blanket spread out.

Math and Music: "The Ants go Marching" – Cut out ten ants from paper and have the children add an ant every time you sing a new verse. Or, they can use their fingers to sing from one to ten. Sing the following song:

(Traditional)
The ants go marching one by one, hurrah, hurrah
The ants go marching one by one, hurrah, hurrah
The ants go marching one by one,
The little one stops to suck his thumb
And they all go marching down to the ground
To get out of the rain, BOOM! BOOM! BOOM!

The ants go marching two by two, hurrah, hurrah
The ants go marching two by two, hurrah, hurrah
The ants go marching two by two,
The little one stops to tie his shoe
And they all go marching down to the ground
To get out of the rain, BOOM! BOOM! BOOM!

The ants go marching three by three, hurrah, hurrah
The ants go marching three by three, hurrah, hurrah
The ants go marching three by three,
The little one stops to climb a tree
And they all go marching down to the ground
To get out of the rain, BOOM! BOOM! BOOM!

The ants go marching four by four, hurrah, hurrah
The ants go marching four by four, hurrah, hurrah
The ants go marching four by four,
The little one stops to shut the door
And they all go marching down to the ground
To get out of the rain, BOOM! BOOM! BOOM!

The ants go marching five by five, hurrah, hurrah
The ants go marching five by five, hurrah, hurrah
The ants go marching five by five,
The little one stops to take a dive
And they all go marching down to the ground
To get out of the rain, BOOM! BOOM! BOOM!

Motor Skills: Tablecloth – Using a large, cheap plastic tablecloth (from the discount store), glue or tape picnic foods cut out from magazines onto the tablecloth. I usually tape two large plastic tablecloths together to make it extra large and for more fun. Instruct the children to jump or hop from food to food on the cloth. Or have them jump to a food that you name and they can stand on one foot on that certain food. This helps them practice balancing. You can also have them walk backwards from food to food or crab walk.

Science: Napkin Experiment – Have the children color on a napkin with markers. Use a spray bottle to spray the color. Talk about their observations and how when the color gets wet, it "bleeds" and the colors can mix together. They can use this same process on coffee filters too.

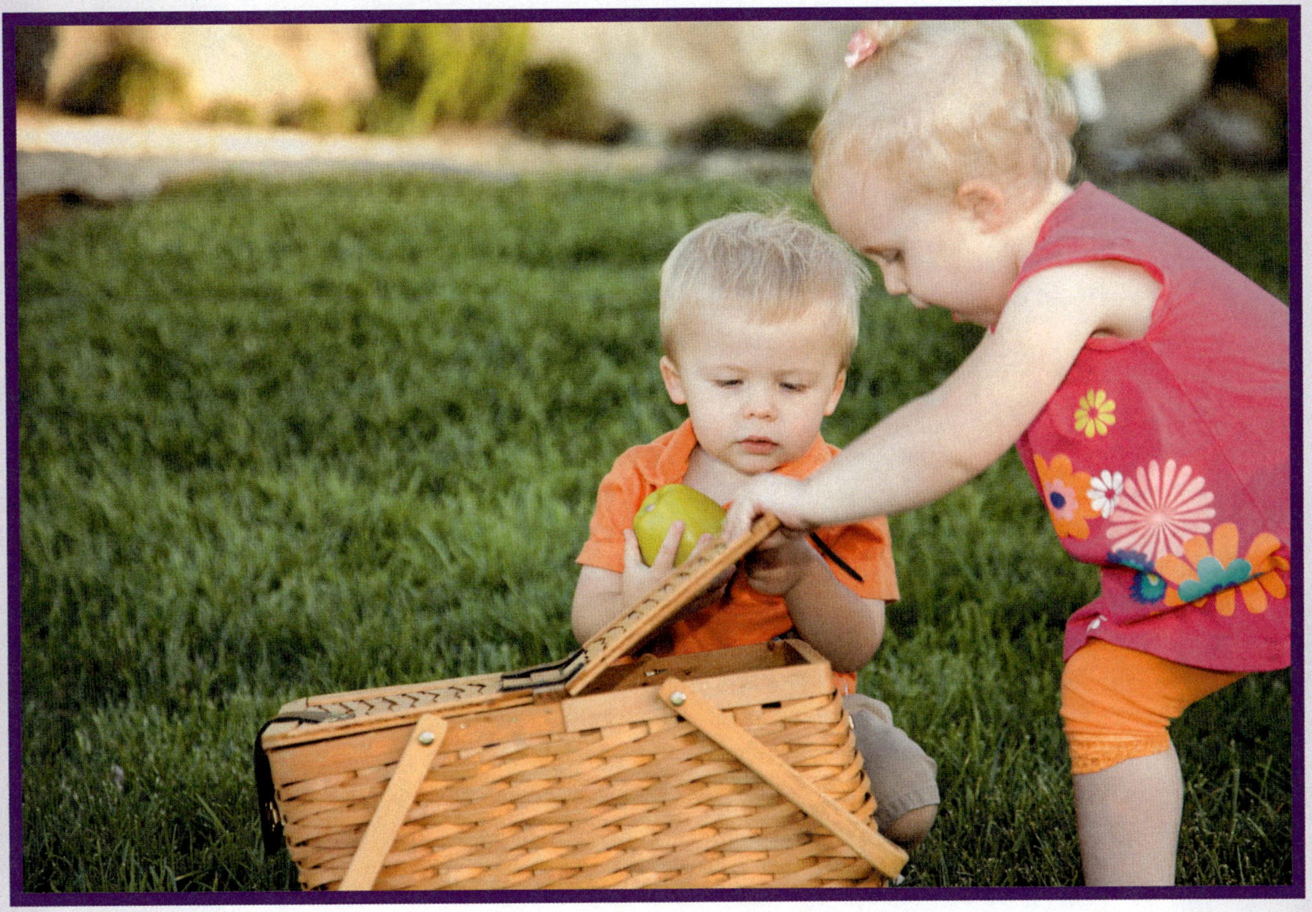

Theme: Summer

Art: Sand Pictures – Either collect sand from the beach (brought home in a ziplock bag) or buy colored sand from the craft store. The children can draw a picture with glue and sprinkle sand over the top.

Cooking and Music: Provide children with a yummy snack of watermelon while singing this song:
"Watermelon"
(Tune: "Are you Sleeping?")
Watermelon, watermelon.
Oh so sweet! Oh so sweet!
Red and green, red and green.
What a treat! What a treat!

Language and Social Studies: Summer Clothing – Talk to the children about appropriate and inappropriate clothing to wear during warm weather. Cut out pictures of the clothing from magazines to glue onto the paper. For appropriate; you might choose sandals, sunglasses, bathing suits, shorts, and tank tops. For inappropriate; you might choose heavy coats, earmuffs, jeans, and boots. Hold up each picture and have the children tell you if the picture describes warm weather clothing or cool weather clothing.

Math: Seashells – Give the children several seashells to look at. Ask the children if they know where they can find seashells. Give them a couple of sand buckets each labeled with a construction paper numeral between 1-10 taped to the bucket. For older children who can count well, you could put the numerals even higher. The children can count the number of seashells to place in the proper bucket. Also teach them how to estimate. Ask them, "How many seashells do you think it takes to fill this bucket?" They (and you!) can take a guess and then help them count how many actually fill the bucket.

Motor Skills/Sensory: Sand Play – Spread newspaper all over the floor and place a large bucket of sand over the newspaper for the children to play in. Provide them with shovels, funnels, and buckets to practice scooping and pouring. You could also do this is the sandbox if they have one at home, or in the sand at the beach or playground.

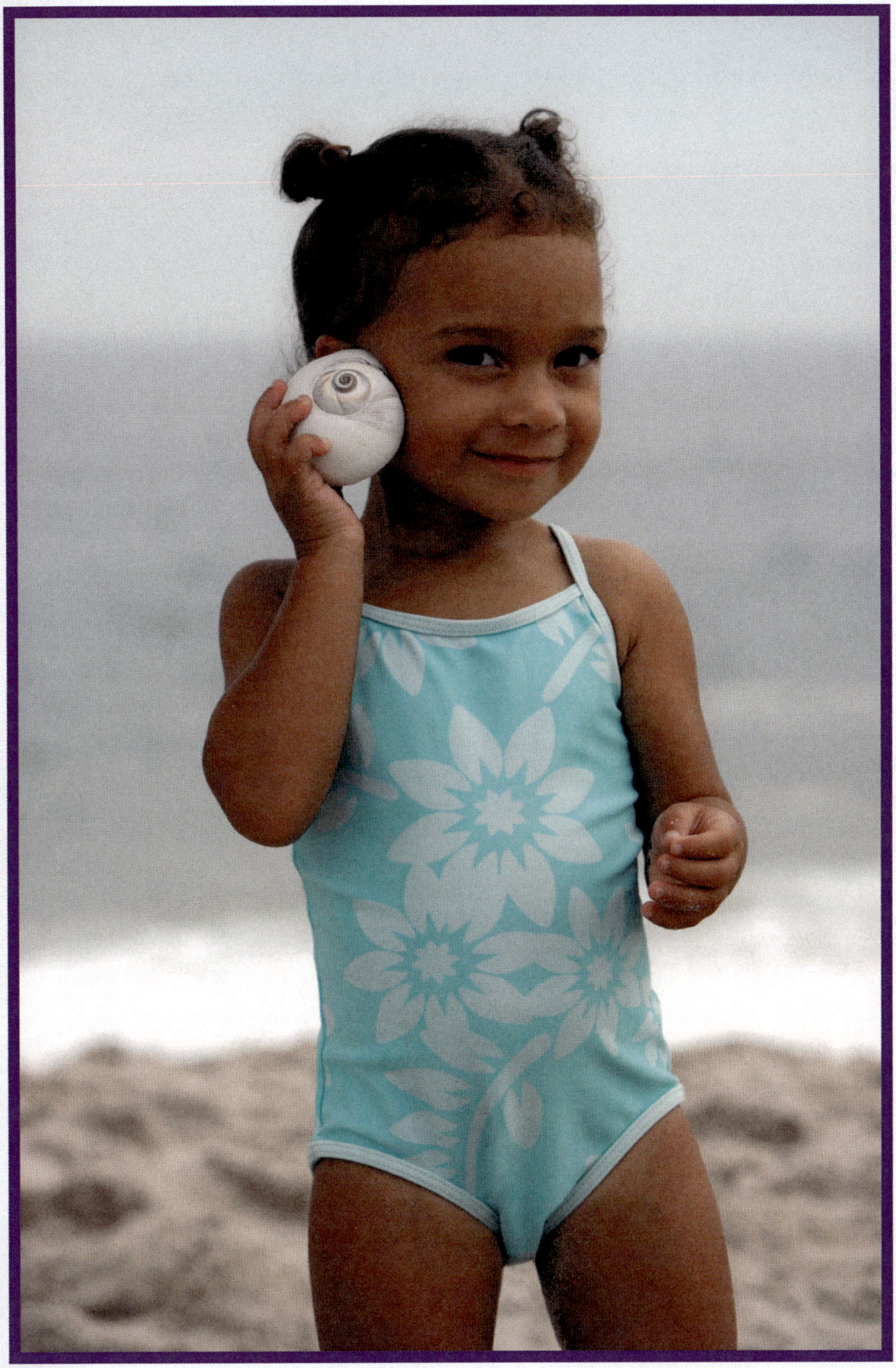

Theme: Daytime and Nighttime

Art and Math: Star and Moon Patterns – Cut out several large moons and stars from construction paper. Use different colors. Have the children use a paintbrush to apply glue onto the stars and moons. Sprinkle glitter onto the glue and allow drying time. Be sure to shake off the excess glitter. Help your charge make a pattern with the stars and moons. They can also sort them by color.

Cooking: Star, Moon, and Sun Sandwiches – Use a star, moon, or sun cookie cutter to press into two slices of bread. Use peanut butter, jam, butter, or egg/tuna salad to spread between the shapes. Eat for snack time. If you do this with grilled cheese sandwiches, you can serve them for lunch!

Language: Daytime and Nighttime Routines – Pull out a sheet of large paper and draw a line down the center of the paper. On one side, draw a sun at the top of the page to represent daytime. On the other side, draw a moon to represent evening. Have the children compile a list of things that occur during the day and at night. For example, during the daytime; they might list things such as going to the park, eating breakfast, riding bikes, or going on playdates. For evening, they might list things such as wearing pajamas, having supper, watching the stars, or catching lightning bugs.

Motor Skills: Star Stickers – Give your charge a sheet of colorful star stickers (you can usually find these for a cheap price at the dollar store). Stick the stars onto black construction paper.

Music: Twinkle, Twinkle, Little Star –
(Traditional)
Twinkle, twinkle, little star.
How I wonder what you are.
Up above the world so high.
Like a diamond in the sky.
Twinkle, twinkle, little star.
How I wonder what you are.

Science: Shadows – Ask your charges if they know what a shadow is. Explain it to them. Take them outside at different points during the day and measure their shadow in one place. Make marks with sidewalk chalk if you can.

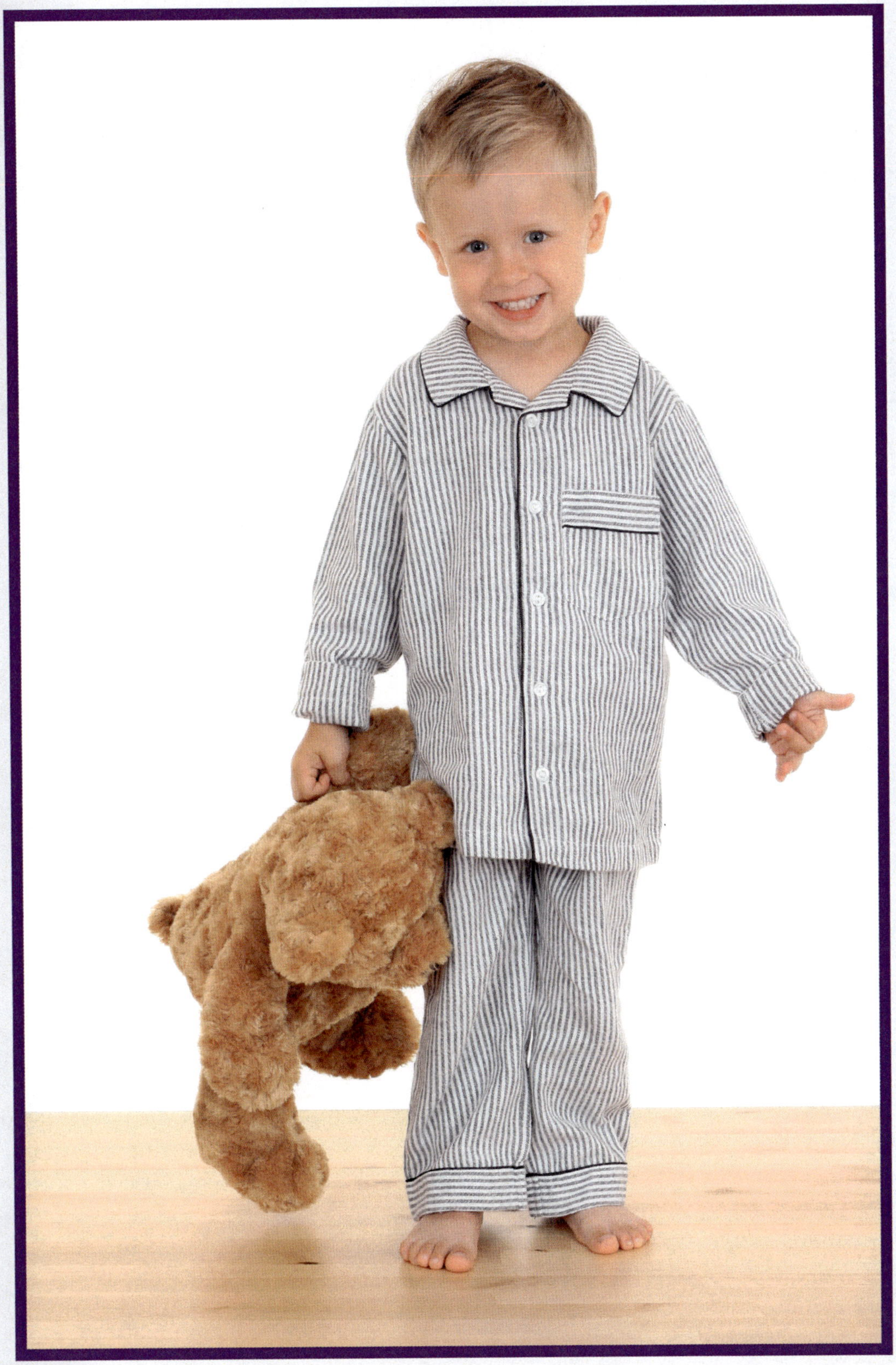

Theme: Fruits

Art, Language, and Science: Fruits Grow on Trees – Explain to the children that while vegetables grow in the ground, fruits go on trees. Have them name some examples of fruit (bananas, peaches, strawberries, apples, etc.). Draw or paint a tree on paper and have the children glue on construction paper fruits on their tree. They could also use fruit stickers.

Cooking: Fruit Salad – Stir together 1 can of pineapple chunks (15 oz), 1 can of fruit cocktail, 1 large container of cool whip, and one package of instant lemon or vanilla pudding. You could also add mini marshmallows if desired.

Math: Sorting Fruit – Use colorful pom-pom balls to represent fruits (yellow – lemons, red – apples, purple – plums, blue – blueberries, black – blackberries, green – grapes, orange – oranges). The children can sort them into piles.

Motor Skills: Pass the Orange – This game is definitely a hit with ages four and up. Use an orange (or a grapefruit) and play catch. The children can practice their throwing and tossing skills. Play on the grass though so the orange doesn't break as easily. Use a hula-hoop for a target to aim into.

Music: "Apples and Bananas"
(Traditional)
I like to eat, eat, eat, apples and bananas.
I like to eat, eat, eat, apples and bananas.

I like to ate, ate, ate, aaples and ba-naanaas. (long "a" sound)
I like to ate, ate, ate, aaples and ba-naanaas.

I like to ite, ite, ite, ipples and ba-ninis. (long "I" sound)
I like to ite, ite, ite, ipples and ba-ninis.

I like to oat, oat, oat, ooples and ba-nonos. (short "o" sound)
I like to oat, oat, oat, ooples and ba-nonos.

I like to ute, ute, ute, upples and ba-nunus. (long "u" sound)
I like to ute, ute, ute, upples and ba-nunus.

Social Studies: Berry Farm – If possible, go to a berry farm and pick berries. Be sure to bring buckets with for picking. Rinse berries well and top them onto cereal or ice cream. Or, dip them into yogurt. Talk to the children about different types of berries. Tell them that while vegetables grow in the ground, fruits grow on trees.

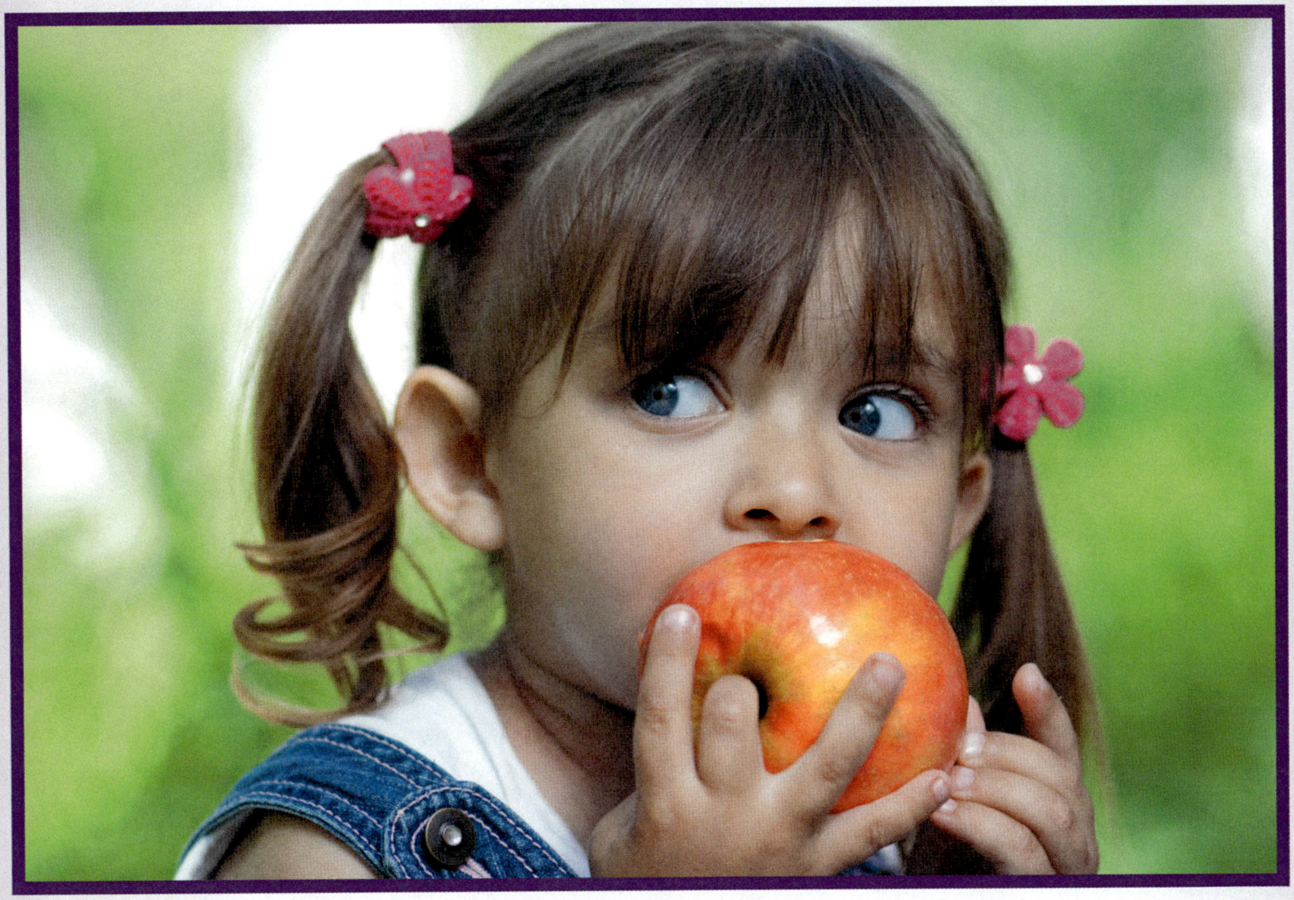

Theme: Feet

Art: Foot Painting – Spread lots of paper all around a section of a room or even outside on the cement. Pour paint onto paper plates. The children should remove their shoes and socks. Dip feet into paint and walk across the paper. You may have to hold your charge's hand as the paint can get slippery.

Cooking: Foot Sandwiches – Use a foot cookie cutter to make foot shapes from your charge's favorite bread. Spread peanut butter on one foot and top with a few banana slices. Place another foot on top to make a sandwich.

Language: Opposites – Read The Foot Book by Dr. Seuss. Help the children understand what opposites are. Give them some of the examples from the book such as left/right, front/back, and high/low. Come up with your own examples too: up/down, inside/outside, long/short, high/low, hot/cold, fast/slow, wet/dry, thin/thick, and sweet/sour. It always helps if you have a visual when teaching young children this lesson.

Motor Skills: Simon Says – Talk to the children about what you can do with your feet. Some answers might be jump, hop, tiptoe, run, walk, wiggle the toes, skip, stomp, and march. Play "Simon Says" and use actions that involve the feet.

Math and Music: Counting Toes – Trace your charge's feet onto construction paper. Count the number of toes and label each toe with a numeral. Sing the following song with your charge:

"Ten Little Toes"
(Tune: "Ten Little Indians")
One little, two little, three little toes.
Four little, five little, six little toes.
Seven little, eight little, nine little toes.
Ten little toes on my feet.

I can jump, I can stomp, I can run too.
I can walk, I can hop, I can tiptoe too.
I can do all these things with my feet.
And I can wiggle my toes too!

Science: Animal Feet – Flip through old catalogs and magazines (or, of course, the internet!) and cut out pictures of animals. Show them to the children and talk about how animals' feet are different from their feet. Discuss their observations.

Social Studies: Podiatrist – Talk to the children about who a podiatrist is and what they do.

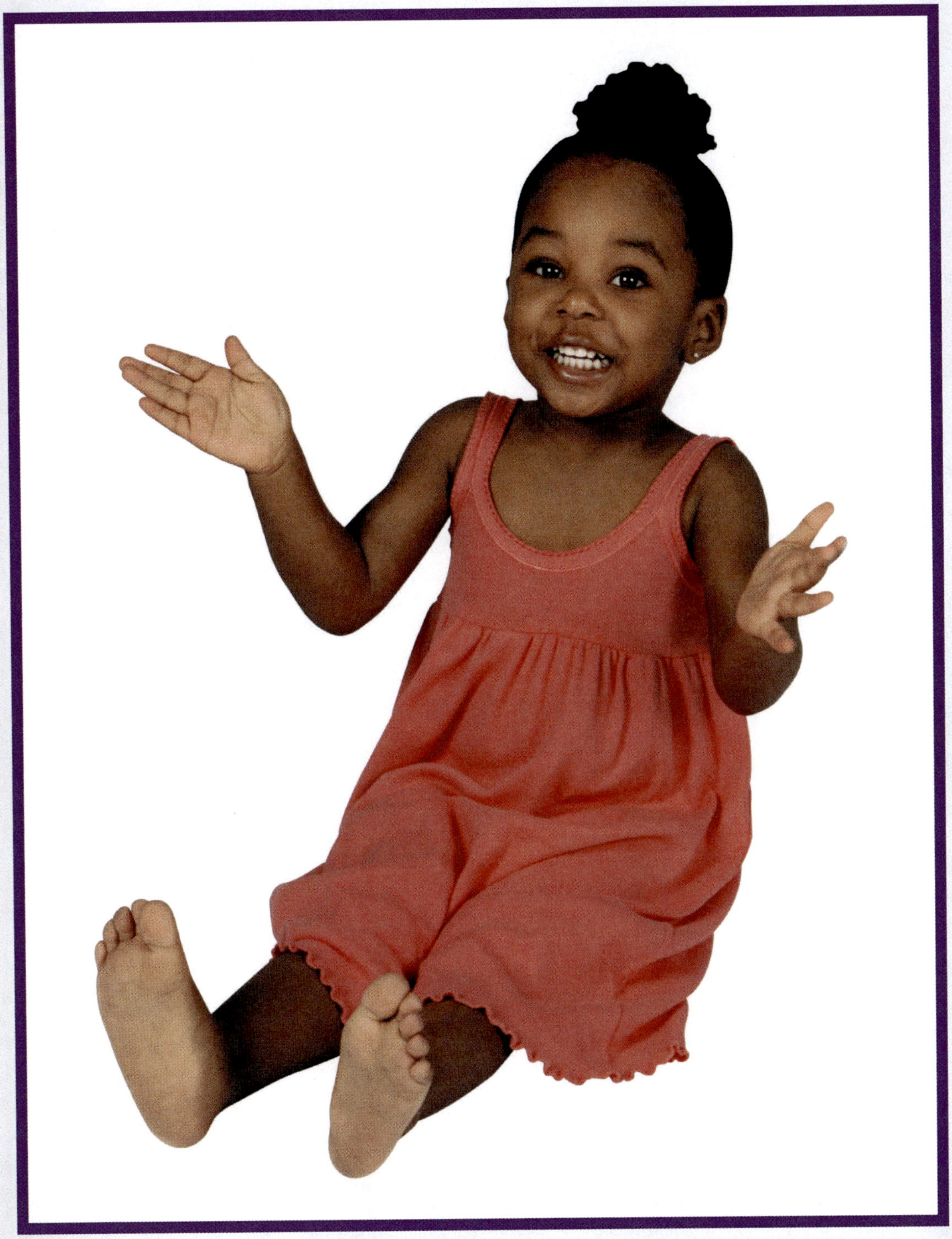

Theme: Pond

Art: Frog on a Lily Pad – Have the children paint a paper plate with green paint. This will be the lily pad. They can also color or paint a picture of a frog. Show them pictures of frogs from a book to show the different types of frogs. Glue the frog onto the lily pad. Finally, glue on a silk or paper flower onto the side of the lilly pad.

Cooking: Pond Bagel – Tint cream cheese with blue food coloring. Spread the blue cream cheese onto half of a bagel. Press goldfish crackers into the cream cheese. Serve for snack time.

Language: Animals in the Pond – Either create or cut out pictures from magazines of a fish, frog, duck, turtle, mosquito, and snail. Place them behind your back and recite the following rhyme:
Look in the pond,
And who do we see?
A _fish_, a pond friend,
Looking at me!

*Hold up the proper picture for each animal you say. Repeat the rhyme replacing the underlined animal for another animal picture.

Math: Counting Bubbles – Cut out ten fish from foam sheets or construction paper. Then cut out 55 blue bubbles. Label each fish with a numeral from 1-10. The children can match the number of bubbles to the numeral on each fish.

Motor Skills: Lily Pad Jumping – Cut out several large lily pads from green foam sheets or construction paper. Spread lily pads all around the room. The children can jump from one lily pad to another. Have them try jumping on two feet and hopping on one foot. Place the lily pads in a circle, line, or zigzag.

Music: "Five Green and Speckled Frogs" –
(Traditional)
Five green and speckled frogs,
Sat on a speckled log.
Eating some most delicious bugs.
Yum! Yum!
One jumped into the pool,
Where it was nice and cool.
Now there are _four_ green speckled frogs.
Glub! Glub!

Repeat replacing underlined number with a decreasing number each time until you are down to one frog. I always like to use felt frogs and a felt log when I sing this song with the children. Great way to incorporate math too!

Social Studies: Pond Field Trip – Take your charges to visit the pond. Bring bread with you to feed the fish and ducks. Take crayons and paper with you and have the children draw what they see. When you get home, talk about their observations.

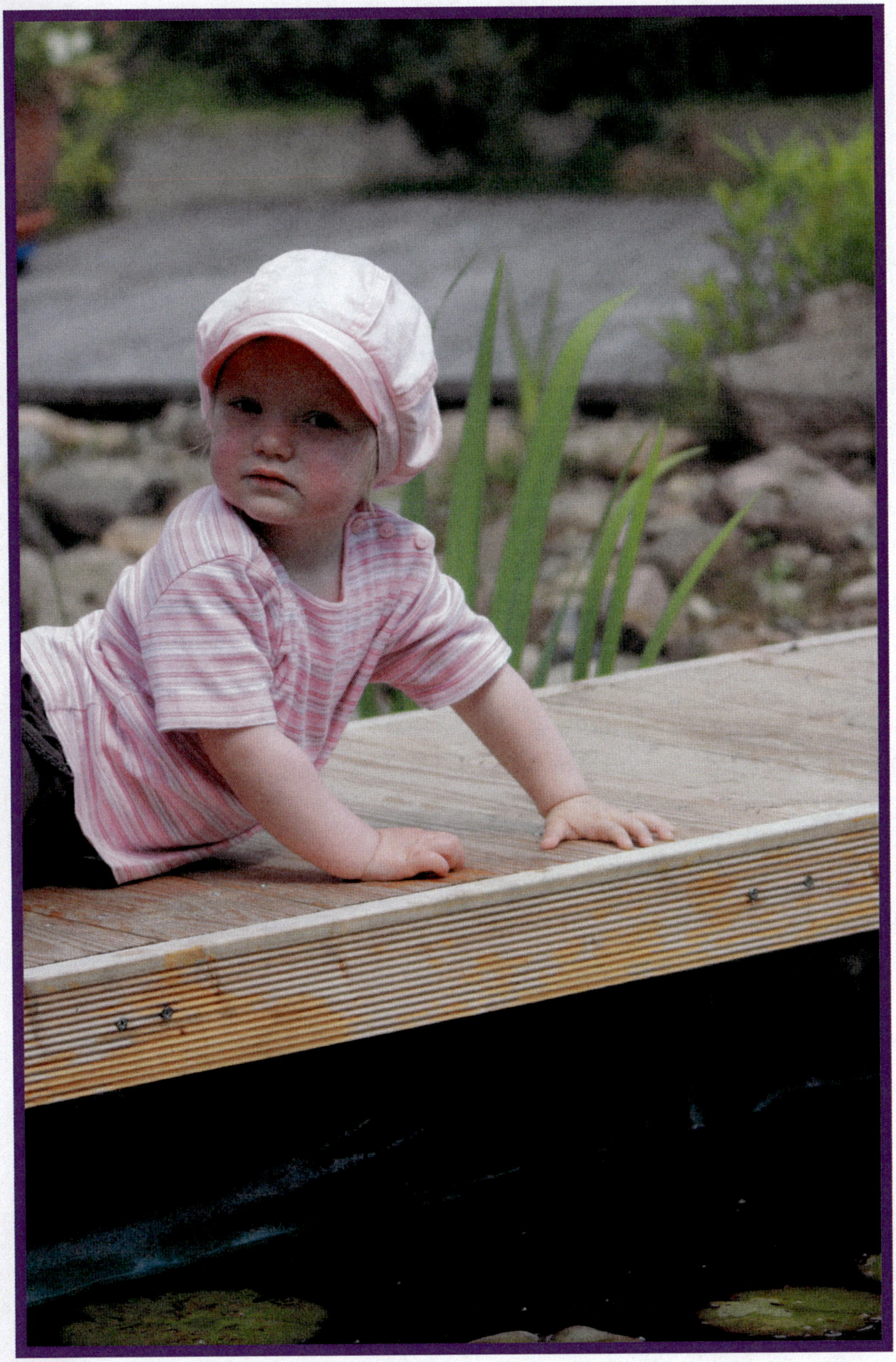

Theme: Feelings

Art, Language, and Social Studies: Paper Plate Faces – Give each child two paper plates. Use markers and wiggle eyes to create a happy face on one plate and a sad face on the other. Glue yarn or string on the top for hair. After the plates have dried, give the children different scenarios and have them hold up which face describes the situation. Some scenarios might include: when they go to a birthday party, when a pet goldfish dies, when someone gets hurt, when someone is sick, when they receive a gift, when mommy and daddy come home, when they go to the park, etc. Also teach them proper words of other types of feelings: jealous, frustrated, scared, angry, proud, silly, and surprised.

Cooking: Toast Faces – Toast a slice of whole wheat bread and spread with peanut butter, honey, or jam. The children can use raisins to create a face on their toast.

Math and Social Studies: Feelings Sort – Flip through magazines and cut out pictures of people showing different emotions (happy, sad, surprised, etc.). Place all of the pictures in a bowl. The children can spread them out on the floor or table and sort them according to emotion.

Music: "If You're Happy and You Know It"
(Traditional)
If you're happy and you know it, clap your hands. (clap, clap)
If you're happy and you know it, clap your hands. (clap, clap)
If you're happy and you know it, then your face will surely show it.
If you're happy and you know it, clap your hands. (clap, clap)
*Repeat song replacing underlined words and actions each time for: stomp your feet (stomp, stomp), jump up and down (jump, jump), and shout "hooray."

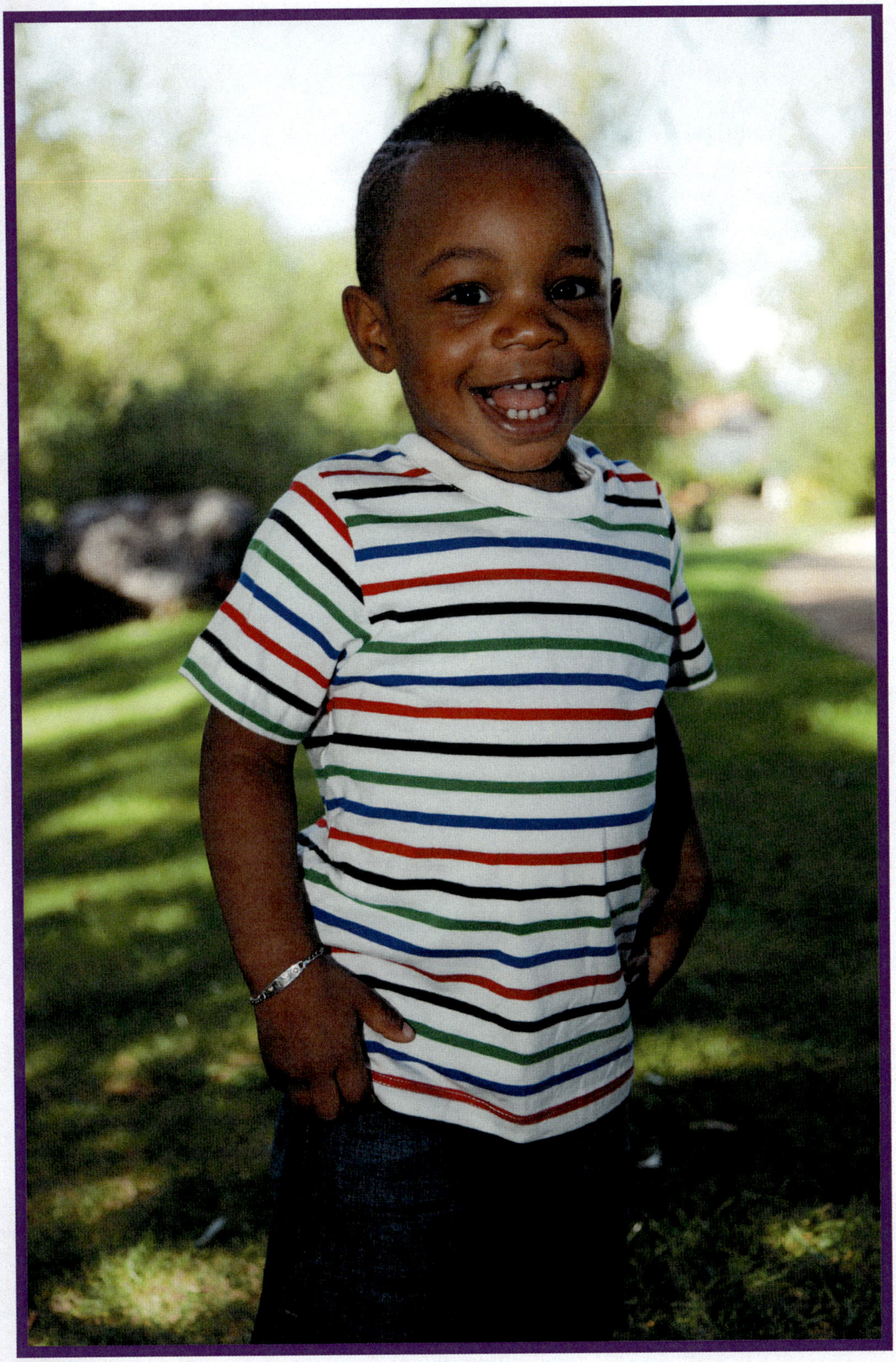

Theme: Apples

Art: Paperplate Apple – Give each child a round white paper plate. The children can paint glue all over one side of the paper plate and sprinkle red tissue paper squares on top of the glue. Add a green stem at the top with a chenille stick. If they'd rather paint instead of gluing on tissue paper, they can fingerpaint the apple red.

Cooking: Homemade Applesauce – Peel, core, and chop 4 apples. In a saucepan; combine apples, ¾ cup water, ¼ cup white sugar, and ½ teaspoon cinnamon. Cover and cook over medium heat for 15-20 minutes or until the apples are soft. Allow to cool and mash with a fork or potato masher. Serve warm or chilled.

Language: "Five Little Apples" – Cut out five apples and tape them to a paper apple tree. Recite the following story:
<u>Five</u> little apples hanging on the tree,
One little apple smiled at me.
I shook that tree as hard as I could.
Down came an apple, (Have your charge take an apple off of the tree)
Mmmmm! It was good!
(Replace the underlined number for a decreasing number each time until there are no apples left hanging on the tree.)

Math: Apple Colors – Explain to the children that apples are not just red. They also come in green and yellow colors. Cut out several apple shapes from red, green, and yellow construction paper or felt sheets. (You can also use real apples for this activity.) The children can sort the apples by color.

Music: "Apples, Apples"
(Tune: "Are You Sleeping?")
Apples, apples.
Apples, apples.
Red, yellow, green.
Red, yellow, green.
Very crunchy.
Very crunchy.
Healthy for me.
Healthy for me.

Science: The Inside of an Apple and Apple Printing – Slice a whole apple in half. Talk to the children about the parts of the apple (the seeds, core, and stem) and how apples grow on trees. Blot the inside of the apple with a paper towel to get rid of the moisture. Pour two to three colors of paint onto separate paper plates (one plate per color). Have the children use a paintbrush to brush paint onto the inside half of the apple. Press the apple onto heavy paper to make apple prints. Dip a small paintbrush into green or brown paint to make a stem at the top of the apple. Let dry and hang for the children to see.

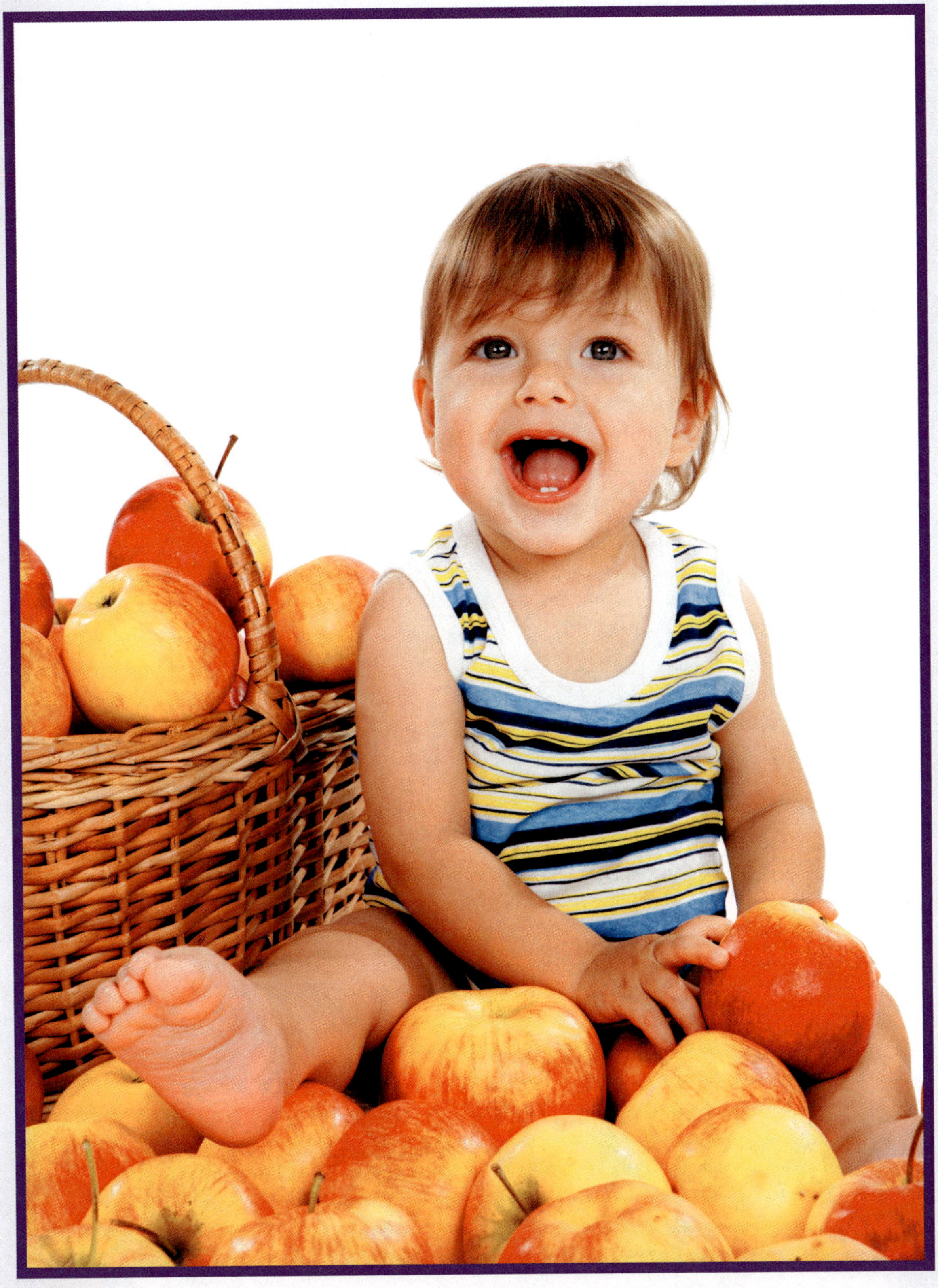

Theme: Pizza

Art and Language: Paper Plate Pizza – Ask the children what kinds of toppings come on a pizza and cut them out of felt. They might name pepperonis, cheese, mushrooms, black olives, ham, pineapple, or peppers. Paint a paper plate red, which will be the pizza sauce. The children can glue the toppings onto their pizza. Yellow or white crinkle paper also makes great shredded cheese. In addition, black pom-poms can be used for black olives.

Cooking: Homemade Pizza – Take the children on a trip to the grocery store to pick up bread dough, pizza sauce, and the toppings that they would like on their homemade pizza. Allow them to help roll the dough, spread on the sauce, and add the toppings. Bake according to bread dough package directions.

Math: Pizza Patterns – Create pizza toppings out of construction paper (pepperonis, black olives, mushrooms, pineapple, ham, etc.). Teach the children how to make patterns with them. (Ex. Pepperoni, olive, pepperoni, olive, etc.) As they get more advanced, make the patterns more challenging. For the older toddlers, start by sorting the toppings into separate piles.

Motor Skills: Pepperonis – Cut out large red circles from construction paper and make a long, winding trail on the floor for the children to follow. The children can practice walking backwards on the trail.

Music: "On Top of My Pizza" –
(Tune: "On Top of Spaghetti")
On top of my pizza
All covered with cheese.
I lost my pepperoni
When somebody sneezed.
AH-CHOO!
It rolled off the table
And onto the floor.
And then my pepperoni
Rolled right out the door.
*Replace underlined word for other pizza toppings such as mushroom, pineapple, black, olive, anchovy, etc.

Sensory: Painting With Pizza Sauce – Allow the children to fingerpaint with pizza sauce on heavy paper. Talk about how the sauce feels.

Social Studies: Pizza Shop – Stop by a local pizza shop and ask if they will give you a few pizza boxes. Add white dish towel "aprons," a pen and pad of paper for taking orders, some fancy placemats and plates; and you'll be all set to play "Pizza Shop!" Create menus for the children to "order from."

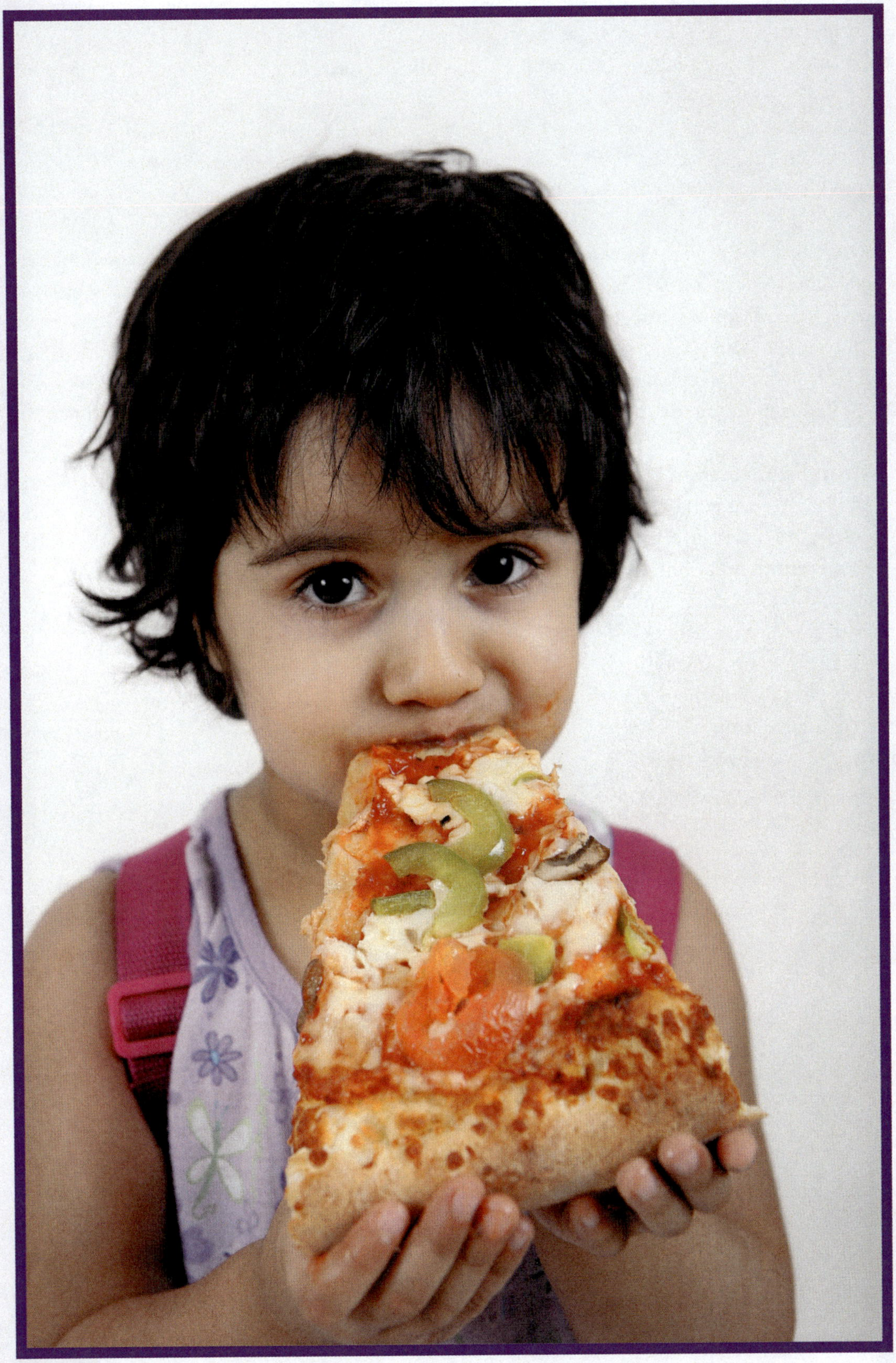

Theme: Fives Senses

Art: A Soft Collage – Talk to the children about the sense of touch. Hunt for things around the home that you can use to make a soft collage such as cotton balls, tissues, pom pom balls, yarn, and old scraps of fabric. Give each child a pile of items to glue on paper in collage form.

Cooking and Science: Popcorn – Using an air popper, the children can watch how the seeds change when they get heated. They can hear the sound of the popcorn popping. Finally, they can smell, touch, and taste the popcorn. Add a little bit of butter if desired.

Language: Feely Box – Cover a shoebox or tissue box with colorful contact paper. If you're using a shoebox, cut a hole into the top of the box that is large enough for a child's hand to fit through. Place an object into the box. Your charge can put her hand in to feel the object. Have her try to guess what's inside. After she guesses, show her what was in the box and then switch the object. Some suggestions for items to put in the box are velvet, cotton, cooked spaghetti, a hard boiled egg, string, or small toys.

Math: Estimating – Using three jars in different sizes, find small household objects to pour into the jars such as jellybeans, buttons, bouncy balls, pom-poms, small plastic bugs, or noodles. Your charges should use their eyes to guess how many objects are in each jar. Record their answers. Help them count the objects in the jar to see how close they were.

Music: "My Five Senses"
(Tune: The Wheels on the Bus")
See with your eyes and smell with your nose.
Taste with your mouth and hear with your ears.
Finally, use your hands to touch.
I use my five senses everyday.

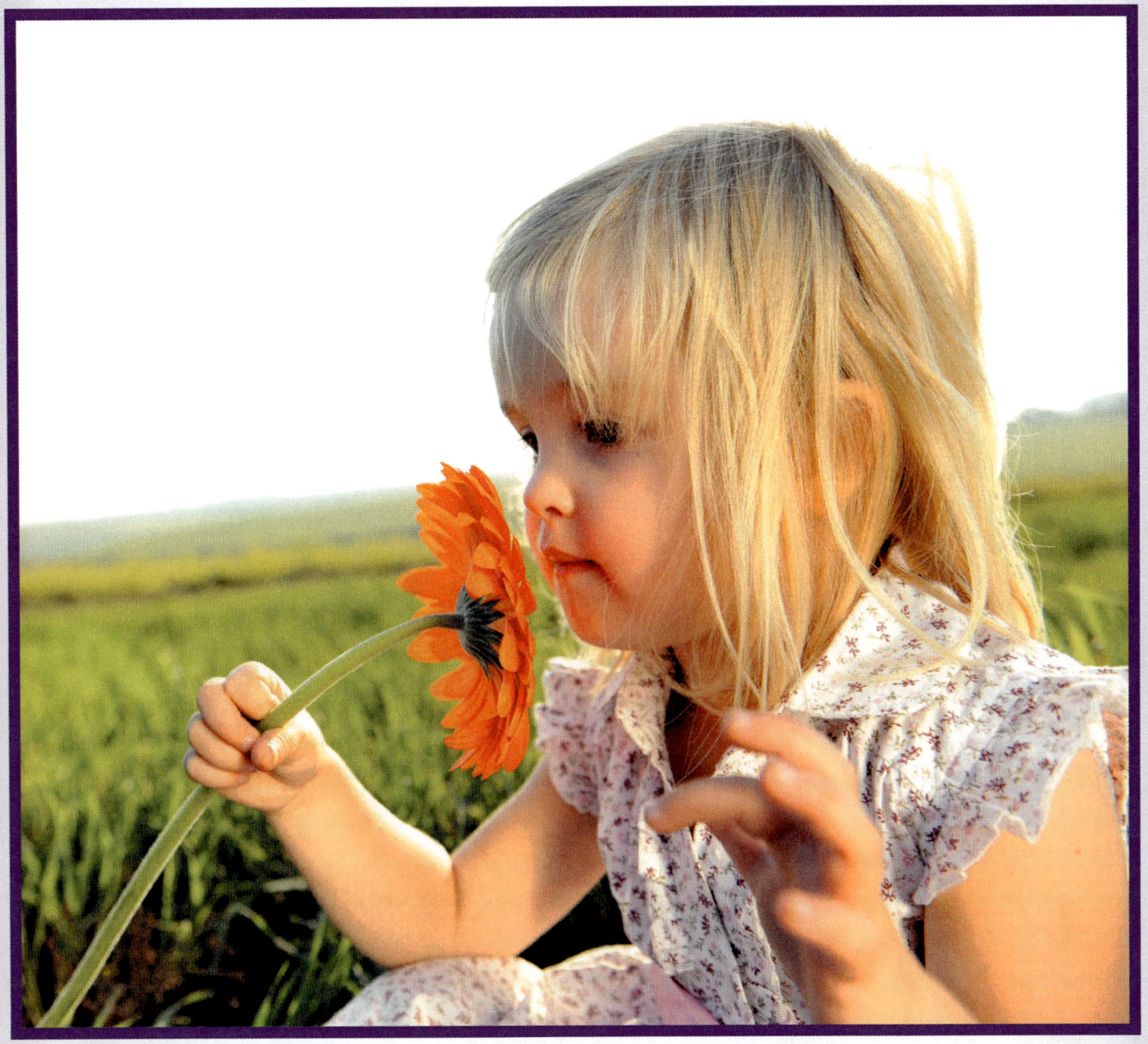

Theme: Leaves

Art: Fall Tree – Cut a large tree shape out of heavy paper. The children can glue silk leaves all over the tree. Or use real leaves collected from a prior walk outside or a tree from the yard. Discuss how the leaves change colors from summer to fall to designate a change in seasons.

Language: Types of Leaves – Head to the library to find books on different types of leaves (maple, ash, evergreen, oak, pine, and willow just to name a few). Have the children help you make these leaves out of paper or copy them off and cut them out. Glue them onto a sheet of large paper or tagboard. Label each leaf. If your charge is an older preschooler, they can help you print the names of the leaves. Display for all to see and learn from.

Motor Skills: Changing Colors – Talk about how leaves change colors and they can be red, orange, yellow, or green. Make several construction paper leaves of each of those colors. Put the leaves in a line on the floor (space them apart well) and designate a motor skill that they are to do for each color. For instance, for red, they should tiptoe around the red leaf. For orange, they should hop on top of the leaf. For yellow, they should skip around the leaf. And for green, they should run in place on top of the leaf. Pick age-appropriate skills for your charge's age group.

Music: "Leaves are Falling"
(Tune: "Where is Thumbkin?")
Leaves are falling, leaves are falling.
From the trees, from the trees.
Red and green and orange.
Brown and yellow.
Fall is here. Fall is here.

Science: Leaf Rubbings – Collect leaves from outside. Have the children bring them inside and get out their crayons. Place a sheet of paper over a leaf. Gently color over the leaf to reveal the leaf's shape and its lines and veins.

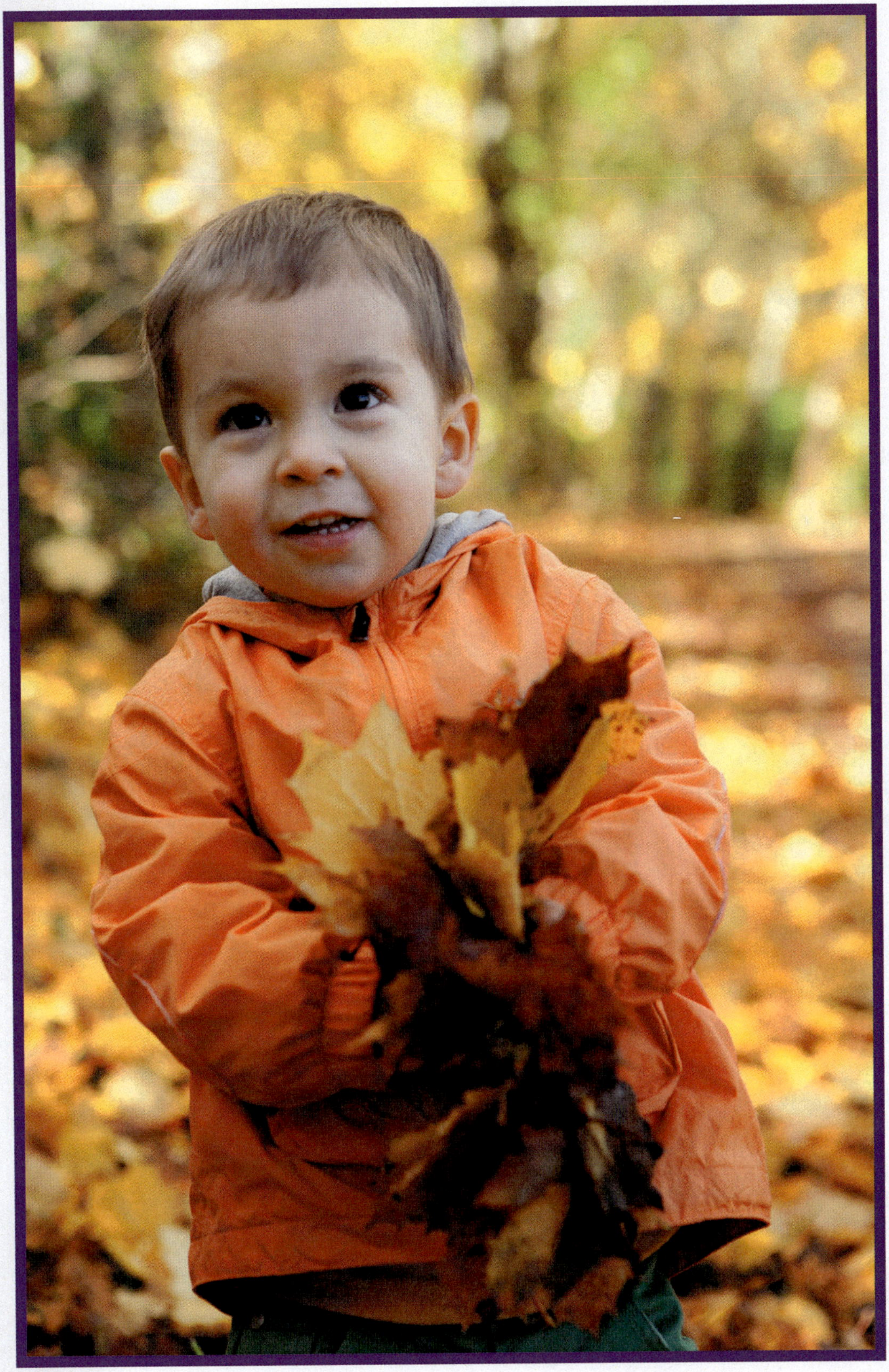

Theme: Pumpkins

Art: Paper Bag Pumpkins – Stuff a small paper bag just over half way with newspaper or paper towels. Twist at the top and secure with a twist tie to make a stem. Paint with a brush or sponge. Make several of these to make a small pumpkin patch!

Cooking: Pumpkin Pancakes – Stir the following ingredients in a bowl:
2 cups flour
2 tablespoons granulated sugar
4 teaspoons baking powder
1 teaspoon salt
1 teaspoon cinnamon
1 1/2 cups milk
1 cup canned pumpkin
4 eggs, slightly beaten
1/4 cup margarine, melted
After the ingredients are all combined together, use to make pancakes as you normally would.

Language and Music: Cut out five different pumpkins from felt or foam sheets. Make one tall, one skinny, one round, one odd-shaped, and one very small. Show the pumpkins to the children and talk about how all pumpkins come in different shapes and sizes. Have the children describe each pumpkin and how they are all different. Hide the pumpkins around the room. Sing the following song while the children try to find the pumpkins:

"Oh Where Have the Pumpkins Gone?"
(Tune: "Oh Where Has my Little Dog Gone?")
Oh where, oh where, have the pumpkins gone?
Oh where, oh where, could they be?
They are tall and skinny,
Round, small, and odd-shaped.
Oh where, oh where, can they be?

Math/Motor Skills: Musical Pumpkins – Cut out several pumpkins from heavy paper. Label each pumpkin with a numeral from one to ten. Cover with contact paper for durability. Spread the pumpkins out on the floor. Explain to the children that when music is playing, they are to walk or dance around the pumpkins. When the music stops, they must find a pumpkin to stand on. When they find a pumpkin, they must jump the number of times written on the pumpkin. This activity is especially fun at a fall party or if the children have a friend over for a playdate.

Science: Exploring a Pumpkin – Carefully cut into the top of the pumpkin. Allow the children to put their hands in and scoop out all of the seeds and pulp. Talk about what you see. Cut eyes, a nose, and a mouth into the pumpkin if desired.

Social Studies: Pumpkin Patch – Take the children to visit a local pumpkin patch. Talk to them about the different sizes of the pumpkins. Collect pumpkins to take home and either carve them or paint them with acrylic paints. If you do not have a pumpkin patch in your area, grocery stores usually have pumpkins for sale.

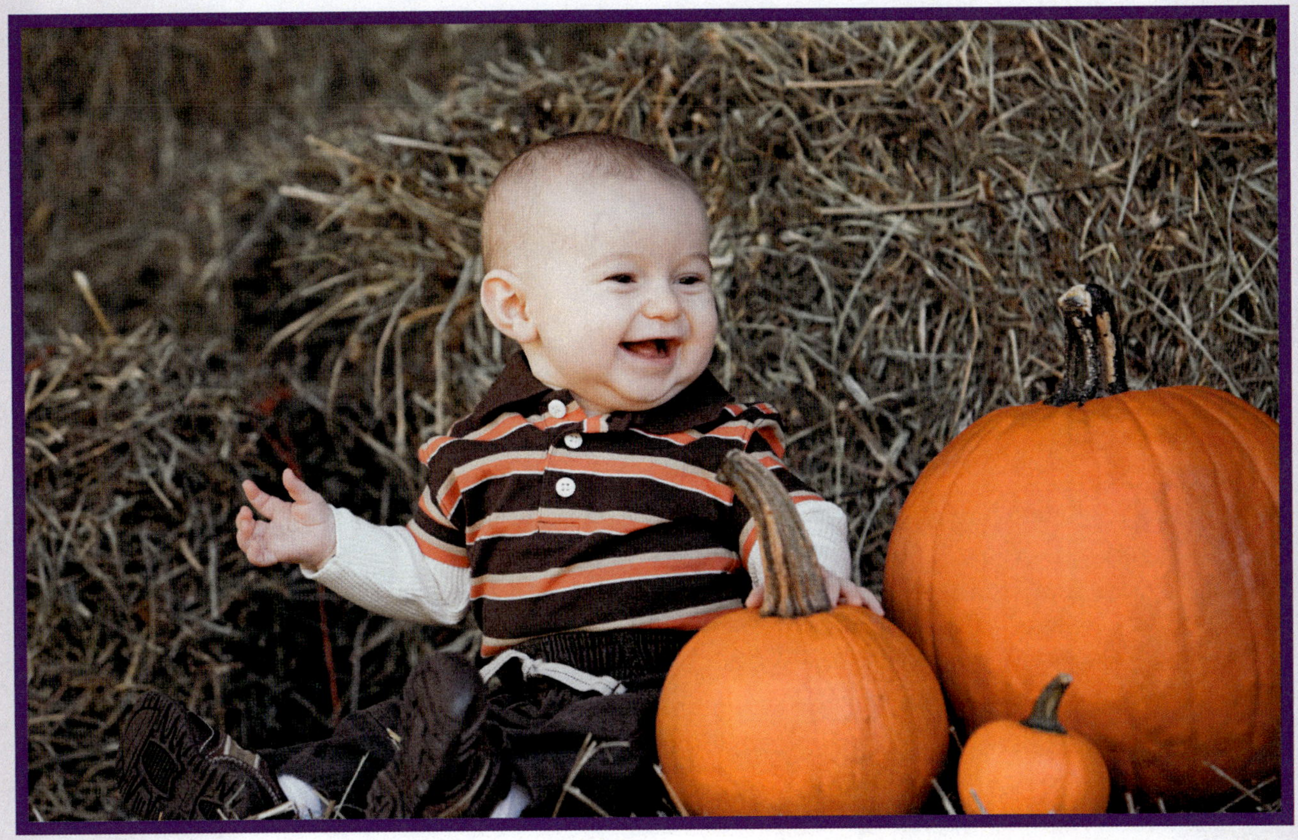

Theme: Red

Art: Red Collage – From the art box, provide the children with red items (yarn, string, glitter, dyed pasta noodles, beads, and textured paper). Have them create a collage with the items. Talk about the materials they are using.

Cooking: Red Raspberry Smoothie – In a blender, toss in one banana, one cup of red raspberries, ½ cup of yogurt, and ½ cup of ice. Blend together and pour into a fun cup for your charge. Add a straw. Serve with crackers.

Math and Science: Shape Sensory Experience - Cut basic shapes from red foam sheets and red textured paper (triangle, circle, square, rectangle, star, heart, oval, and octagon). Have the children name the shapes. Place the shapes in the sand box and hide them. The children can use their hands or shovels to dig for the shapes.

Motor Skills and Science: Rigatoni Necklace – In a ziplock bag, pour ½ cup of alcohol and about 20 drops of red food coloring. Place 1-2 cups of penne or rigatoni noodles into the bag and seal it very tightly. Swish the pasta noodles in the color. Let them set flat on a counter. Flip the bag over every half hour for a couple of hours to make the colors more vibrant. The longer they set, the brighter they'll be. Remove the pasta from the bag and let dry. The children can string the noodles onto string, yarn, or ribbon to make a necklace.

Music: "Red Song"
(Tune: "Three Blind Mice")
Red, red, red.
Red, red, red.
The color of many things.
It's in the rainbow too.
Firetrucks, apples, and roses.
Tomatoes, robins, and strawberries.
Did you also know that red means, "stop"?
Red, red, red.
Red, red, red.

Social Studies: Fire Truck – Talk to the children about fire safety. Teach them the stop, drop, and roll technique. Using the top of an egg carton, the children can use their brushes or a sponge to paint it red. Add black construction paper wheels and a chenille stick "hose." The older children usually like to make a ladder. I always like to add a picture of a Dalmatian dog glued to it.

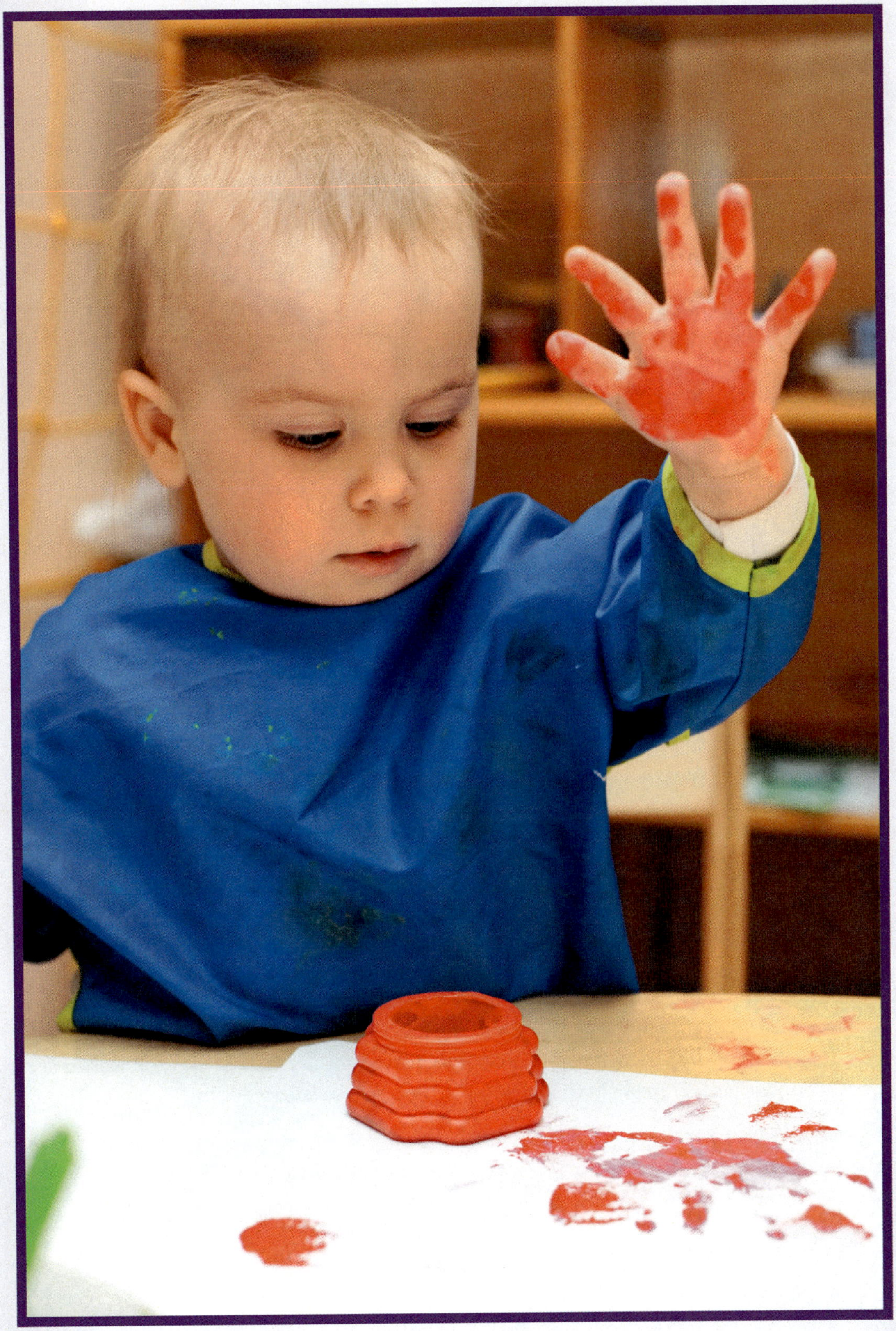

Theme: Farm

Art: Feathered Chicken – Provide children with a cut out of a chicken. You can also find a template online. Spread colored feathers onto the table or in a dish. The children can glue the feathers on the chicken.

Cooking: Homemade Butter – Pour 2 cups heavy cream into a food processor or blender. Blend for ten minutes or until the butter separates and strain off the liquid. If desired, season with ¼ teaspoon salt. Press the butter into a small bowl with the back of a spoon. Spread on crackers, a muffin, or toast.

Language and Math: Big and Small – Collect several toy farm animals or pictures of farm animals and have the children name them. Find as many as you can (turkey, cow, sheep, pig, duck, dog, cat, chicken, goat, horse, etc.) and have the children name them. For this activity, it's best to use adult and baby animals (for example, a cow and a calf, a horse and a colt, or a goat and a kid). The children can then sort the animals into piles of big and small.

Motor Skills: Milking a Cow – Talk to the children about how milk comes from cows. Place wax paper or newspaper all over your work area. Pour tempera paint into a plastic glove. Tie the glove at the top with a rubber band. Make small slits at the ends of the fingers. Hold the glove up for the children (over heavy paper) and show them how to "milk a cow."

Music: "Old MacDonald Had a Farm"
(Traditional)
Old MacDonald had a farm.
E-I-E-I-O.
And on his farm he had a duck
E-I-E-I-O.
With a quack quack here
And a quack quack there.
Here a quack, there a quack
Everywhere a quack quack.
Old MacDonald had a farm.
E-I-E-I-O.
(Replace underlined animal and sound for other farm animals.)

Science: Sensory Experience – Place hay into a large container. The children can hide small plastic or rubber farm animals in the hay. Explain to them what hay is for.

Social Studies: Farm Visit – Many city children have never even been to a farm before. Take the children to a real farm where they can see the animals and duties of a real farmer. Before you go, make a list with them of items and animals they might see at the farm. Take your list with you. As you walk around, the children can cross off the things on the list that they see.

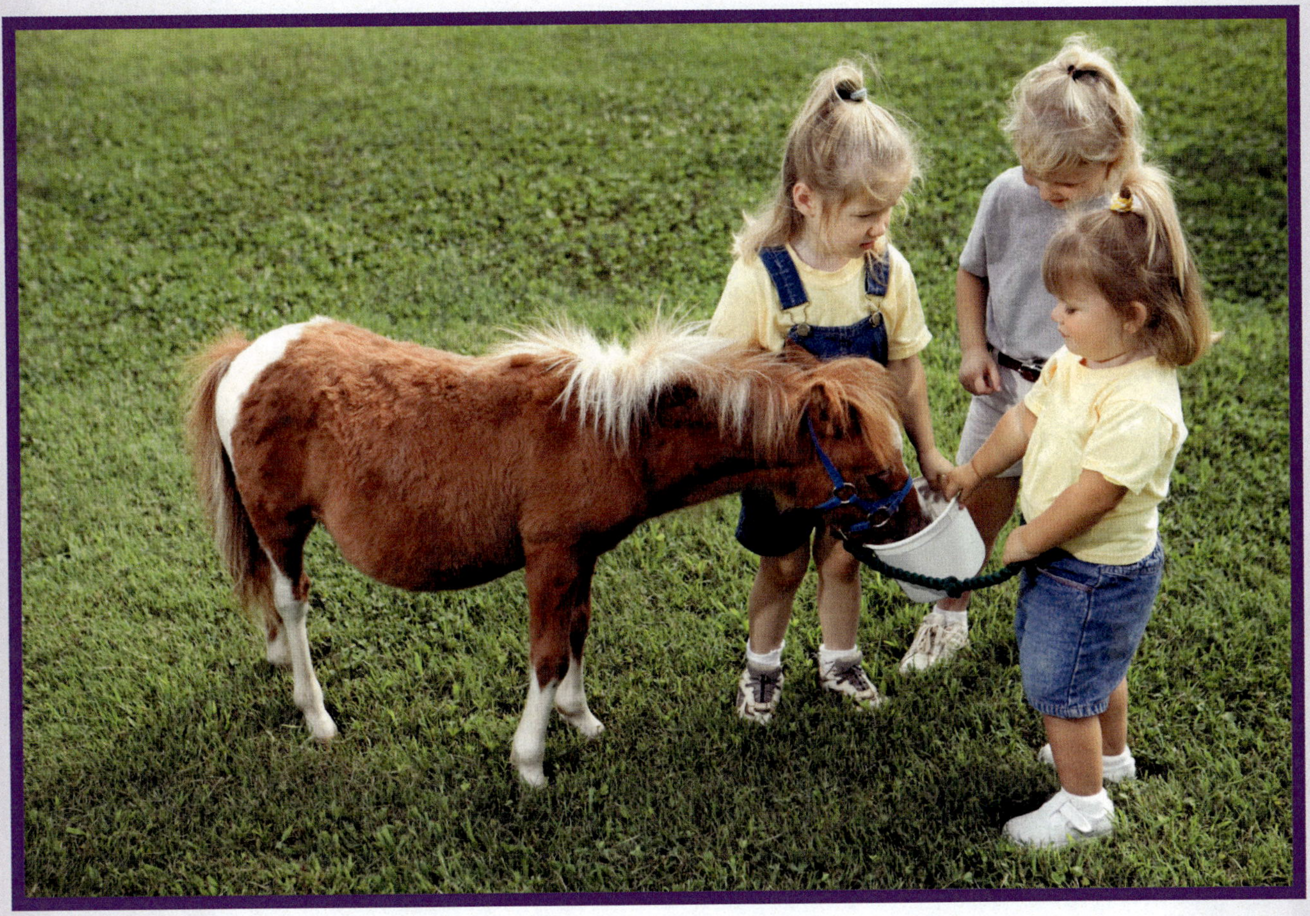

Theme: Vegetables

Art and Motor Skills: Corn Printing – Give each charge a sheet of white paper and pour a considerable amount of liquid paint onto a large paper plate. Teach the children how to roll an ear of corn into the paint and onto the paper to make corn prints. This is good for their wrist development. They can also use large fresh peppers and carrots by slicing them in half (lengthwise) and pressing them into the paint and onto paper.

Cooking: Vegetable Dip – Combine together a 10 ounce package of spinach (drained and thawed), 1 cup mayonnaise, 1 cup sour cream, and one package dry vegetable soup mix. Mix together and chill overnight.

Language: Which Vegetable is Missing? – Use plastic or real vegetables and place them into a bowl or basket. Show the basket to the children and have them name the vegetables. Have the children cover their eyes and remove one of the vegetables. See if the children can guess which one is missing. Older toddlers can start with three or four vegetables. For preschoolers, add more.

Math: Measuring Carrots – Provide the children with either precut construction paper carrots or long carrots bought from the grocery store. Help them to use a tape measure to tell how many inches long they are. They can also line them up according to their size.

Music: "Vegetables Song"
(Tune: "Twinkle, Twinkle, Little Star")
Radishes, spinach, potatoes too.
Carrots, beans, and broccoli, just to name a few.
These are all vegetables which grow in the ground.
They need lots of water and sun all around.
Eat lots of veggies at dinner and lunch.
Chew them up and hear them go crunch, crunch, crunch.

Science and Social Studies: How Vegetables Grow – Explain to the children that vegetables grow in the ground. Provide them with a picture list of vegetables (carrots, green beans, peas, turnips, beets, carrots, lettuce, etc.). Visit the grocery store with their list in hand and have them circle the vegetables that they see as you are shopping. Let them pick out a couple of vegetables that they would like to try at home or buy the ingredients for making vegetable dip (recipe shown above).

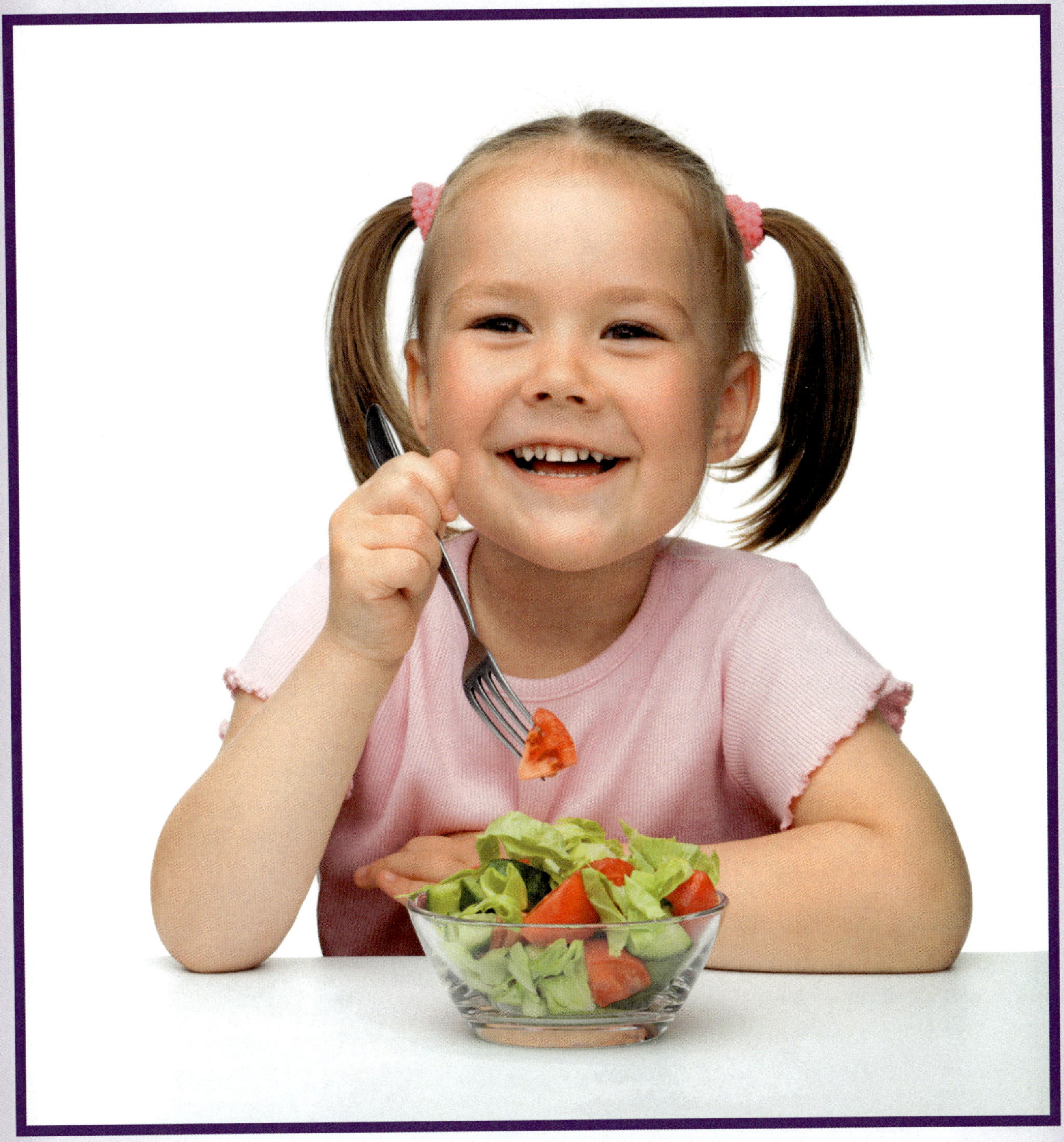

Theme: Mittens

Art: Mitten Set – Cut out two mittens for each child from heavy paper or cloth. The children can decorate them as they desire. Use rick-rack, yarn, or glitter glue. Attach a long rope to the mittens.

Cooking: Hot Cocoa – Combine 1/3 cup unsweetened cocoa poser, ¾ cup white sugar, 1 pinch of salt, and 1/3 cup boiling water in a saucepan. Bring this to an easy boil while you stir. Simmer and stir for about two minutes. Watch so that it doesn't scorch. Stir in 3-1/2 cups of milk and heat until very hot, but do not boil. Remove from the heat and add ¾ teaspoon vanilla extract. Allow to cool in serve in mugs for the children. If the children are old enough, drop a few mini marshmallows into the mug as well.

Math: Mitten Match – Gather several mittens from the coat closet and place them into a pile. You can also cut out several paper mittens from heavy paper, felt, or foam sheets. Make sure every mitten has a match. Help the children to match the mittens. For older toddlers and young preschoolers, start with just three or four sets. As they progress, you can add more.

Motor Skills and Science: Snow – Bring a large bucket of snow inside and put it into a large container or in the bathtub. The children can put their mittens on and play in the snow! Provide them with scoops, shovels, and containers to mold the snow into.

Music: "Mittens Song"
(Tune: "Bingo")
I have two mittens upon my hands
To keep them toasty and warm
M-I-T-T-E-N (clap for each letter)
M-I-T-T-E-N
M-I-T-T-E-N
My mittens are so warm!

Social Studies: Warm and Cold Climates – Provide the children with pictures of different environments – snowy, sunny, the beach, a mountain, and countries that are warm all year round. Ask your charges what we use mittens for (to keep our hands warm). Help them to understand that not all places get cold. Some places are warm year-round, therefore, people do not need to wear mittens.

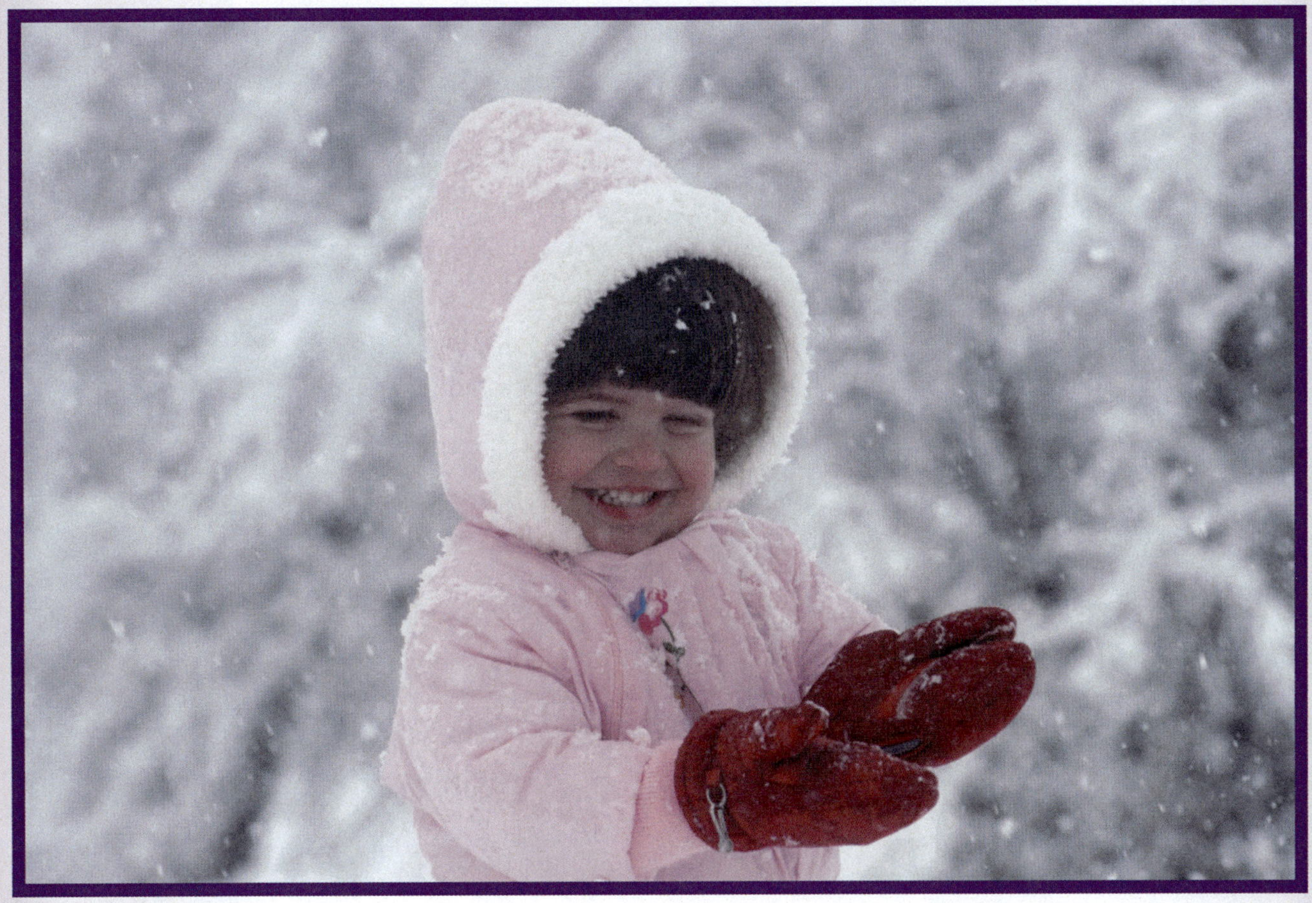

Appendix A:

Early Academics

Learning early academics works wonderfully with children over the age of two being taught one-on-one in a home environment. Keep in mind that all children are different so some may be ready sooner than others, while others may not be ready until later on. Incorporate learning early academics into their everyday life. If you are sitting at the table having lunch, you might say something such as, "You have yellow corn on your plate." Or, "Your bowl is the shape of a circle." If you are taking a walk outside, you might point out the letters on the stop sign as you pass by it. Play "I Spy" with the children by saying "I spy something green." Then, the children try to guess what you are looking at. If you are putting away toys, you might count the number of red blocks that you put back into the toy bin. You could also pick a letter of the week (or shape, number, or color) and do a few activities relating to the letter. Last week, I introduced the letter "M" with my 2-1/2 year old charge, whom has had such a fascination with letters lately. Some of our activities included baking muffins, creating a collage with pictures of objects cut out from old catalogs that start with the letter "m," and I put several household objects in my nanny surprise bag that started with "m" which he pulled out and named (mittens, a toy mouse, mixing bowl, milk carton, maracas, etc.). Through these activities, he developed language skills, a nutrition and cooking lesson, and fine motor skills.

There are countless toys that teach from early on about shapes, colors, letters, and numbers. There are also many great picture books available which teach all of this stuff too. However, as far as the actual teaching goes; shapes and colors should come first. They can start being taught at around eighteen months. Followed by letters and numbers, which can start being taught when the children are about 2-1/2 to three years of age. I always believe that the whole writing process starts around the age of four years. Many children even begin before. All things develop in a sequence; therefore, don't just think to yourself, "Oh, he's three years old. This means he's ready to write now." It's always about when the children are ready. Allow your infants and toddlers the opportunity to scribble a lot which will help to contribute to the writing process as well. Be sure to do small muscle skills activities and fine motor skills activities with your charges which will help with writing skills and learning to control a pencil.

When I use the word "teach," I do not mean sitting your charge down at the table and actually giving them instructions on how to memorize and write shapes, letters, colors, and numbers. These "academics" should never be pushed. Never force your charges to complete worksheets to draw shapes or write letters or numbers. Same goes for flashcards. They will have plenty of time for worksheets and flashcards when they get into school and by forcing them to do it will only cause them to get frustrated, give up, and just plain hate it. In fact, I wouldn't even suggest or encourage utilizing worksheets and flashcards with them at this age.

Sometimes I will choose a letter, number, shape, or color as the weekly theme for my charge (just like a theme from the thematic curriculum). No matter what type of curriculum you are choosing to do for the week, add early academics activities into the day every once in a while. I have created my early academics curriculum to be just like any other curriculum. All of the activities have a purpose and come from one of the curricular areas.

For alphabet letters, some of the activities can be the same idea for each letter. Here are some examples:

- Social Studies – Pick an occupation, which starts with the letter. Talk about what the job is. It's always a good idea to have a picture of the person performing the job (or in uniform) in which you are talking about to show the children. Tell them about the job in simple terms. And, of course, if it is possible, visit the place of work. Remember that children are visual learners.

- Science – Collect pictures of animals, which start with the letter and show them to the children. You can go to almost any search engine (google.com is my favorite!) and type in an animal or word, then click on "images," and pictures of what you typed in will show up. Then, you can print them off. Cover them with contact paper for durability.

- Language – Assist your charge in cutting out pictures from old catalogs and magazines. Glue and label them onto heavy paper for a collage of items, which start with the letter you are teaching them about. Or, use a nanny "surprise bag" and place a few objects that start with the letter in a special bag and the children can pull out one object at a time and name the object. This is an excellent way to enhance their vocabulary and language development. Otherwise the easiest way to enhance their language and vocabulary is to print off pictures from the computer or cut out pictures from magazines that start with the letter and show them to your charges.

- Music – I have a special song that my charges and I like to sing. It is to the tune of: "Zippity Doo Dah."

Zippity Doo Dah,
Zippity Day.
My, oh my, let's name some L words today.
Ladybug, light bulb, and laugh too.
Zippity doo dah, zippity day!

109

LETTER A:

Words for the children to learn: Apple, Anchor, Arm, Autumn, Apron, Acorn, Airplane, Ax, Award, Arrow

Animals: Alligator, Ant, Antelope, Armadillo, Ape

Occupation: Astronaut

LETTER B:

Words for the children to learn: Bicycle, Book, Ball, Big, Backpack, Bat, Balloon, Bus, Bread, Bricks

Animals: Bear, Bumblebee, Bunny, Bird

Occupation: Baker

LETTER C:

Words for the children to learn: Car, Cake, Can, Carrot, Cup, Cone, Chair, Chimney, Cheese, Chain

Animals: Camel, Cat, Caterpillar, Chameleon, Chicken, Clam, Chipmunk, Cow, Colt, Crocodile, Cheetah

Occupation: Chef

LETTER D:

Words for the children to learn: Drum, Dirt, Daisy, Donut, Dart, Doll, Dime, Dice, Dance, Dump Truck

Animals: Dog, Donkey, Dolphin, Dragonfly, Deer

Occupation: Doctor, Dentist

LETTER E:

Words for the children to learn: Eight, Egg, Eye, Earth, Ear, Eat, Easel, Earmuffs, Erase, Envelope

Animals: Elephant, Earthworm, Eagle, Emu, Eel

Occupation: Engineer

LETTER F:

Words for the children to learn: Fern, Fan, Feather, Fire, Fork, Feet, Family, Flag, Flute, Flower

Animals: Fish, Firefly, Frog, Fly, Flamingo

Occupation: Farmer, Firefighter, Florist

LETTER G:

Words for the children to learn: Grapes, Gate, Gift, Guitar, Garbage, Golf Club, Girl, Gingerbread, Grapefruit, Grass

Animals: Giraffe, Gorilla, Goat, Goose, Grizzly Bear, Groundhog

Occupation: Golfer

LETTER H:

Words for the children to learn: Hat, Heart, Hanger, Hairbrush, Hands, Hill, Ham, House, Hammer, Head

Animals: Horse, Hippopotamus, Hamster, Hen, Hawk

Occupation: Hairdresser

LETTER I:

Words for the children to learn: Igloo, Icicle, Ice Cream, Ice Skates, Island, Ice, Iris, Ink, Iron, Ivy

Animals: Iguana, Inchworm, Insect

Occupation: Ice Skater

LETTER J:

Words for the children to learn: Jump, Jellybean, Jam, Jacket, Jet, Jar, Jewelry, Jeans, Jumprope, Jug

Animals: Jellyfish, Jaguar, June Bug

Occupation: Jet Pilot, Juggler

LETTER K:

Words for the children to learn: Kite, Key, Kazoo, Kayak, Kettle, King, Kick, Knife, Keyboard, Knot

Animals: Kangaroo, Koala, Kitten

Occupation: Karate Instructor

LETTER L:

Words for the children to learn: Leaf, Lollipop, Lemon, Lobster, Log, Lips, Lamp, Light Bulb, Ladder, Lake

Animals: Lamb, Ladybug, Lion, Lynx, Llama, Leopard

Occupation: Librarian

LETTER M:

Words for the children to learn: Money, Mittens, Muffin, March, Map, Mushroom, Moon, Man, Milk, Magnet

Animals: Mouse, monkey, moose

Occupation: Mailman

LETTER N:

Words for the children to learn: Nail, Notebook, Net, Nose, Nest, Newspaper, Needle, Notebook, Numbers, Neck

Animals: Nightingale, Narwhal, Night Crawler

Occupation: Nurse

LETTER O:

Words for the children to learn: Octagon, Oatmeal, Oboe, Onion, Oval, Oar, Orange, Olive, Open, Over

Animals: Ostrich, Owl, Octopus, Ox, Otter

Occupation: Oceanographer

LETTER P:

Words for the children to learn: Pocket, Pencil, Pear, Pin, Pail, Pliers, Peach, Pizza, Pot, Plant

Animals: Penguin, Pig, Platypus

Occupation: Photographer

LETTER Q:

Words for the children to learn: Queen, Quilt, Quarter, Quiet, Quiver, Question Mark, Quadruplets, Quart, Question

Animals: Quail

Occupation: Quilter

LETTER R:

Words for the children to learn: Rose, Rain, Ring, Rainbow, Rake, Rectangle, Racket, Robot, Rock, Rope

Animals: Rat, Raccoon, Rhinoceros, Reindeer, Rabbit

Occupation: Radio Announcer

LETTER S:

Words for the children to learn: Sailboat, Sock, Sandals, Stapler, Stool, Stump, Shorts, Shampoo, Shot, Scarf

Animals: Snake, Seal, Starfish, Sheep, Skunk

Occupation: Scientist

LETTER T:

Words for the children to learn: Taxi, Tooth, Train, Tractor, Trombone, Tree, Table, Tomato, Tent, Thermometer

Animals: Tiger, Tadpole, Toad, Turtle, Tarantula

Occupation: Teacher

LETTER U:

Words for the children to learn: Umbrella, Up, Unicorn, Unhappy, Upside-Down,

Underwear, Unicycle, Utensils, Under, Uncle

Animals: Unicorn, Uria

Occupation: Upholsterer

LETTER V:

Words for the children to learn: Vest, Volcano, Vacuum, Vote, Violin, Van, Vegetables, Vase, Vote, Vine

Animals: Vulture, Viper

Occupation: Veterinarian

LETTER W:

Words for the children to learn: Wagon, Wheel, Wand, Woman, World, Watermelon, Web, Whistle, Wisk, Wall

Animals: Whale, Wasp, Walrus

Occupation: Writer

LETTER X:

Words for the children to learn: X-Ray, Xylophone

Animals: Xenops

Occupation: X-Ray Technician

LETTER Y:

Words for the children to learn: Yarn, Yo-Yo, Yam, Yacht, Yolk, Yell, Yogurt, Yellow, Yardstick

Animals: Yak

Occupation: Yoga Instructor

LETTER Z:

Words for the children to learn: Zigzag, Zipper, Zero, Zucchini, Zoo, Zinnia, Zither

Animals: Zebra

Occupation: Zookeeper

115

Appendix B:

Lessons on Health, Safety, and Nutrition

It is vital that children learn about health, safety, and nutrition. The following are key topics that should be discussed with them in a developmentally appropriate manner:

- Buckling a Seatbelt
- Covering a Cough
- Crossing the Street
- Exercise
- Fire Safety – Stop, Drop, Roll
- Handwashing
- Healthy Foods
- Knife Safety
- Red = Stop, Green = Go
- Scissors Safety
- Strangers
- Toothbrushing
- Going to the Doctor
- Going to the Dentist
- Calling 9-1-1
- The First-Aid Kit
- Using Soap
- Saying "Excuse me"
- Blowing and Wiping Your Nose
- Protection from the sun
- Poison
- Taking Medicine
- Appropriate Seasonal Clothing
- Stop Signs
- Hot and Cold Water
- A Hot Stove
- Holding onto the Railing (Stairs)
- Matches
- Safe and Dangerous Items for Play
- Smoke Detectors
- Keeping Fingers Away from Doors
- Holding Hands While Crossing the Street
- Safety Around Animals
- What to do if You are Lost
- Knowledge of Name, Address, and Phone Number
- Food Groups
- Setting the Table

Acknowledgments:

Wow! I can't believe I'm already on the acknowledgments page! It's hard to believe this book is finally finished after hours spent behind the computer! There are several people I would like to thank:

Mom and Dad – Thank you for always encouraging me to go for my dreams. You have taught me the importance of a good work ethic, how to remain confident, and most importantly - how to be humble. I love you!

The Garner Family – Alexander, Emma, Max, Charlie, and Grace – Thank you for allowing me to be a part of your family. Words cannot even begin to express my truest gratitude.

My child development professors, Marsha and Jamie – Thank you for your guidance, examples, and role modeling.

Fatima Aderogba – You are a true friend and an inspiration. Thank you for all of your help, direction, and for answering my questions.

Jessica, Jasmine, and Kaitlyn – I could have never made it to New York City without your support! xoxo.

My past nanny families and all of the children, fellow teachers, nannies, and agents that I have had the opportunity to work with – I am very privileged to have had so many magnificent opportunities and experiences both in the classroom and home environments.

Thank you, God…. for answering my prayers!

Max and Grace

Charlie

Max

Charlie, Grace, and Max - 2013

Acknowledgments:

Wow! I can't believe I'm already on the acknowledgments page! It's hard to believe this book is finally finished after hours spent behind the computer! There are several people I would like to thank:

Mom and Dad – Thank you for always encouraging me to go for my dreams. You have taught me the importance of a good work ethic, how to remain confident, and most importantly - how to be humble. I love you!

The Garner Family – Alexander, Emma, Max, Charlie, and Grace – Thank you for allowing me to be a part of your family. Words cannot even begin to express my truest gratitude.

My child development professors, Marsha and Jamie – Thank you for your guidance, examples, and role modeling.

Fatima Aderogba – You are a true friend and an inspiration. Thank you for all of your help, direction, and for answering my questions.

Jessica, Jasmine, and Kaitlyn – I could have never made it to New York City without your support! xoxo.

My past nanny families and all of the children, fellow teachers, nannies, and agents that I have had the opportunity to work with – I am very privileged to have had so many magnificent opportunities and experiences both in the classroom and home environments.

Thank you, God…. for answering my prayers!

Max and Grace

Charlie

Max

Charlie, Grace, and Max - 2013

My amazing parents- Ken and Peg Laubenthal

Jessica, "Aunt" Patty, Jasmine, and I

Made in the USA
Middletown, DE
16 September 2022